The Intangible Investor

Profiting from Intellectual Property:
Companies' Most Elusive Assets

The Intangible Investor

Profiting from Intellectual Property: Companies' Most Elusive Assets

By Bruce Berman

ISBN-13: 978-0615952352

Other Books by Bruce Berman

From Assets to Profits
Competing For IP Value & Return

Making Innovation Pay
People Who Turn IP into Shareholder Value

From Ideas to Assets
Investing Wisely in Intellectual Property

Hidden Value
Profiting from the Intellectual Property Economy

Chapter:

The Book of Investing Rules
Invaluable Advice from 150 Master Investors

For Benjamin Graham, who reminds us that
before there were intangible investors, there were intelligent ones.

Content

Foreword

For the past 15 years I have been writing articles and commentaries in the hope of educating those new to the intellectual property world about the counter-intuitive characteristics that comprise the U.S. patent system. Intellectual property generally, and patents specifically, are among the most important assets most companies own. Yet the public knows little about the importance of employing an exclusive rights system for innovation, and most senior business executives and seasoned investors are befuddled by it. Their choices can cause those with more intimate IP knowledge to scratch their head in disbelief.

It will not come as a shock to observers of the U.S. businesses that manufacturing is no longer the focal point of the economy. Indeed, the continuous trend is toward an innovation and technology-based economy where intellectual property rights, particularly patents, rule the day. To paraphrase Bruce Springsteen — the manufacturing jobs are gone and they ain't coming back.

Prosperity in the United States is now almost completely tied to innovation and a prerequisite to successful innovation, access to capital. The central theme of Bruce Berman's new book of timely essays, *The Intangible Investor*, focuses on the issues surrounding our innovation economy: capital, valuation and leveraging IP for business advantage. The domain of intellectual property and intangible assets is very different from the bricks and mortar world inhabited sophisticated investors and business executives. Unlike real estate, intangible assets are not scarce, can be infinitely replicated and wholly divided. That makes monetizing the handful of patents that have value a formidable challenge.

This book is a collection of short, memorable articles that focus on teaching a particular issue or aspect of intellectual property, often dealing with patents. Specifically, *The Intangible Investor* confronts head on the importance of acquisition and the myriad issues in play during licensing and enforcement proceedings. Berman's approach to teaching through vignettes makes the patent systems many nuances easier to understand

and the topic more approachable for diverse audiences.

One of the most remarkable things about this collection is how these essays have weathered the test of time. While the 64 essays in *The Intangible Investor* stretch back to 2003, they are as relevant today as they were when they were written, which is a testament to Berman's forward thinking and deep understanding of the issues.

Illegitimate assertions?, written in 2004, starts by stating that: "Patent trolls have been all over the news lately... " which is undeniably as true today as it was a decade ago. But even in these early days of the so-called patent troll problem, Berman was keenly aware that there was more than meets the eye, something that continues to elude many policy makers on Capitol Hill and journalists. He explained back in 2004 that the ability to assert patents is critical to any patent holder, but that large corporations with substantial patent portfolios were surprisingly vulnerable to being sued by holders who do no manufacturing themselves. Today, corporations still are unable to crack this code, rendering Berman's observation both relevant and eerily prophetic.

Another example of Berman's insight comes from a 2006 piece titled *Skin Deep*. Here he discusses patent quality, which has been an issue in the patent community with respect to software and information technology patents since at least 2002. It continues to be an issue today because patents issued in the era where quality was lower than it is today are still being litigated. In fact, the patents from this "low quality era" at the USPTO will still be litigated for years to come.

In *Skin Deep*, Berman makes the observation that patent quality is not the same as patent value. Indeed, a patent can be quite valuable when the quality is very low (and worth nothing when it is high). In fact, some patent attorneys will try to secure claims that are very broad, knowing full-well that they are unlikely to survive. It is a strategy designed to secure both solid patent claim coverage while at the same time sprinkling in nebulous, ill-defined, perhaps even ridiculously broad claims, which may cause other businesses problems. This is done because challenging a patent that has issued is expensive and for that reason and others pursuing litigation is often imprudent. It also means that with alarming frequency licenses are taken (and paid for) on patents that are of dubious meaning.

Viewed collectively the contributions in *The Intangible Investor,* aptly subtitled, "Profiting from Intellectual Property: Companies' Most Elusive Assets," provide managers, entrepreneurs and investors interested in intellectual property, as well as IP professionals, with useful intelligence on how the industry works, and a historical context for what it means. The fact that the industry has yet to deal with the many thorny problems that began to surface just about a decade ago means these essays remain as fresh as they are informative. Those serious about obtaining a fuller understanding of the IP system will find it impossible to come away from *The Intangible Investor* without actionable intelligence and a better awareness of the issues, the first step in leveraging information for a higher return.

I wholeheartedly recommend reading *The Intangible Investor,* and congratulate Bruce Berman for his long standing commitment to making the intangible IP system more intelligible to investors and other audiences.

Gene Quinn
Editor, IP Watchdog
U.S. Patent Attorney

Introduction

We live in dangerous times for new ideas. The rights that protect inventions, patents, once regarded as obscure legal documents, have come to represent the best and worst that innovation has to offer. While rights are seen by some as an emerging asset class, others believe they are road blocks. Both are partially right.

Patents today are not what the Founding Fathers had in mind when they were written into the Constitution of the United States in the late 18th century. At the time, the power to grant inventors a period of exclusivity in exchange for disclosing their discovery was a bold idea. Led by James Madison, the framers of the Constitution were prophetic in envisioning how IP rights could generate value for the nation as it grew, and for creative individuals and young businesses.

The Intangible Investor is a collection of perspectives written over the past decade that cover how intellectual property rights, especially patents, have come to be used to generate return.

This book has multiple purposes: (1) to provide the many audiences affected by IP a basis for understanding how it can generate value, (2) to help readers better discern what is meant by patent "quality," and who, in fact, are the IP system's bad actors, and (3) to provide a context to discern the developments that have taken place over the past decade in IP in the hope of better equipping us for the ones ahead.

There are good reasons for presenting these previously published pieces in book form. After reviewing the body of work, more than 60,000 words, they are a lot less cringe-worthy than expected. In fact, they hang together pretty well. Taken as a group these essays are cohesive in ways they cannot be when read as bi-monthly contributions to a magazine. Reading them in rapid succession felt to me a little like binge-watching several seasons of "Breaking Bad." They are reminiscent of the collections of film reviews that were abundant in the 1960s and 1970s in book form and that provided an expanded frame work for reflection.

The Intangible Investor is not only intended for IP professionals and patent holders. It is a resource for anyone affected by the business of innovation or interested in making sense of it. It is best read in several sittings to get a better handle on how IP rights generate return and how patent quality, often in the eye of the beholder, also is subject to legal qualifications. People that will benefit from this book include shareholders, employees, inventors, private equity investors, law-makers, mothers, journalists, holy men, academicians, CEOs and government regulators.

Despite patents' higher profile, many audiences see them today as impediments; a toll plaza slowing traffic on the innovation super-highway that restricts good products from reaching the widest audience at the lowest price. Others regard patents as an incentive, and among the few options available to small companies, universities and independent inventors that level the playing field. The power of patents and the intentions of patent holders have been hotly debated and are broadly misunderstood. Both have fared poorly in the Court of Public Opinion. Several of the chapters in *The Intangible Investor* examine why.

Yours, mine, ours

Many of us are intangible investors – unseen stakeholders with an interest in what is provided by patents and other innovation rights, intangible assets by accounting definition. While IP rights may be owned by individuals or assigned to companies, how they are deployed, and by whom, is what gets people most riled up. The preceding decade's challenge was to discern "how are IP rights assets?" For the coming one it will be "how can IP rights best be used to support innovation?"

Contrary to popular belief, patents do not protect inventions. A patent is no little more than a hunting license, or, to put it even more bluntly, the right to sue. It entitles the holder 100% of something that in practice amounts to nothing 98% or more of the time. Like a mining claim, an issued patent often looks much better on paper than it does in practice. Trial-quality patents are surprisingly few and far between.

When corporations own them, they are seldom enforced even when infringed for fear of harming customers, vendors and even competitors.

A patent holder cannot dial 911 and say, "Arrest that man, he's stealing my invention!" Enforcing patents is not the responsibility of local or federal police, or state militia. Suits are extremely expensive, time consuming and risky, even under the best circumstances. A patent suit affords the holder the opportunity to attempt to force an infringer to take a license or, in the rare instances if a dispute gets to trial and wins likely appeals, to collect damages.

Invention disputes are inevitable. How they get resolved is not. While patent trials are often in the headlines, they are relatively rare, with fewer than 150 occurring annually. The rapid growth of innovation over the past twenty years assures disagreements, so does the growing number of newly issued patents and the value of patent-reliant products, like smart phones. Given their underlying R&D cost and lack of reliability it is a wonder there are not tens of thousands of patent suits annually and hundreds of trials. Contrary to what you read, most patent suits are not frivolous or generated by so-called patent "trolls" (a bogey man admittedly dreamt up by an Intel litigator in 2001 to re-frame how a dispute was characterized in the press). Patent suits often are brought because most infringers refuse to negotiate a license unless they must. Ninety-five percent or more settle. The numbers of patent cases that are brought in the U.S. annually are a fraction of the 276,788 patents that were granted in 2012. A significant part of the problem is that many patents are unreliable and probably would not have been issued in the first place had the USPTO sufficient examination resources. The best of those patents that issue are more valuable to some businesses than others. Profiting from them is highly relative.

If the high cost and extended timeline of patent suits sounds like a license For infringers to steal ideas from undercapitalized businesses' and confused inventors, it is not far off. Despite this some patent holders are able to prevail over much larger and better-financed rivals, a testament to the power of American ingenuity and the patent system.

As the playing field for patent holders has leveled somewhat over the past 30 years, it has not stopped those used to its advantages from attempting to retain them.

Separating truth from fiction in today's IP world is an obsession of mine. It also is a theme woven into *The Intangible Investor*. I hope that this book will help readers realize that distinguishing the good actors from the bad in IP is not as easy as it might look. Condemning patent enforcement and demonizing all non-practicing licensors may be an acceptable storyline to lazy reporters. Often disputes have more to do with a business' failure to address all of its innovation needs internally, and its motivation to avoid paying for using what others' own unless forced to.

From frames to claims

The book is arranged chronologically, beginning with, *Who owns IP?*, written in 2003. This structure provides the most organic way to observe the progression of themes and topics over time. For readers who resist consecutive reading, it is fine to begin where your interest takes you, and proceed from there. *The Intangible Investor* represents 63 columns published in IAM Magazine beginning in July 2003 and stopping in January 2014. (I thought about including some unpublished material, however, those of you familiar with, *IP CloseUp* (**www.ipcloseup.com**), the blog I began publishing in 2010, know where to find additional information.) Beginning in the middle of the book may be helpful to some, and for those I urge an initial reading of "A curious journey," in which *IP Investor* is rechristened *The Intangible Investor*. Here, I discuss how a lowly Columbia cinema studies instructor (me) went from analyzing movie frames to considering invention claims. Looking back it makes more sense than I would have imagined some 40 years ago. It also explains how the column came to be, and how Benjamin Graham, the renowned value investor worshipped by Warren Buffett, played a part.

Another good place to begin is at the 50th column, *0 to 50 in 8.5 years*. It is sometimes difficult to tell which parties are most responsible for the "gaming" system: Those who file poorly researched patents to puff up their portfolio count; acquirers of questionable patents that prey on risk-adverse business that settle suits to avoid high cost of defense; or companies that systematically practice other's inventions because they have calculated that (given the high cost of litigation) there is a slim likelihood of being caught. All of them are bad for innovation.

Depending on the industry in which they do business, established companies typically use their patents differently from young businesses, independent inventors or NPEs, a fact that readers of *The Intangible Investor* are familiar with. Truth be told, many large tech companies that stockpile patents believe that they have more to lose than gain from strong patents. They would not mind if lawmakers and the courts could find a way to neutralize them. These companies practice a tiny percentage of the patents they hold and are suspicious of the good ones they do not.

A few words about the text – All chapters are reproduced as originally published, in Anglicized English by way of London-based IAM, except for a few places where I felt compelled to change a word, phrase or punctuation for clarity. All chapters are under 1,000 words, making it relatively easy to peruse *The Intangible Investor* as in print form or as an eBook. A few columns deal with content or copyright issues, especially as they relate to the Internet, counterfeiting and trademarks or brands. I believe that IP rights issues frequently are intertwined and issues affecting copyright holders or brands overlap with patent and trade secret matters.

No matter how well we might prepare for the future it will likely take us by surprise. The future of IP will be no different. Unreliable as it is hindsight beats groping in the dark. Looking back on IP business matters of the recent past provides context and some clues. What I am told that I do well – and what few patent attorneys, inventors and managers are trained to do – is explain how patents and patent strategies provide value.

Fifteen or twenty years ago, getting a business editor to run a patent story was like subjecting him to surgery without anesthesia. "How am I going to sell it to my editor?" was a familiar response. Today, editors have difficulty keeping trash-talk about patent trolls off of the front page. At last count, there are some seven patent-weakening, anti-monetization bills before the U.S. House and Senate designed to make good patents less valuable and incensing and enforcement more difficult than they already are. Those bills voted into law will not necessarily have a positive impact on innovation.

I hope *The Intangible Investor* helps readers realize that when it comes to IP rights to generating a positive return for businesses, individuals and society there are as many shades of black and white as there are of gray.

Bruce Berman
New York City
2014

The best time to plant a tree was 20 years ago. The second best time is now.

Chinese Proverb

Who owns IP?

2003

As intellectual property moves to the centre-stage of business concerns, there is a growing need for senior executives to devise and then implement successful IP management strategies. Investors expect nothing less.

More people have a business interest in intellectual property than they realize. Only some are aware of it. Patents, copyrights, brands and other intangible assets are too important today not to care about. Business decisions need the guidance of patent counsel, but they also require the input of R&D, licensing executives and investment bankers. Even more important, they need the vision and leadership of informed senior management.

"IP has got to be on the CEOs' radar screen as something worthy of their attention," Nicholas Godici, USPTO Commissioner for Patents, told a diverse group of IP experts at a Washington, DC roundtable recently. "Frankly, what we have not seen in Washington are CEOs stepping up to the plate to show that they are actually aware of intangible assets and the need to identify their importance. Either they are unaware of the problem or are uncomfortable discussing it."

As Godici suggests, an appreciation of the role patents play in attaining overall business objectives currently evades most senior managers. Understanding the subtle interplay between innovation, law and markets only looks like rocket science. Those with a vested interest in IP need to participate in decision-making. Key players should include senior management, especially CEOs and CFOs, as well as company directors and financial advisors.

Two decades ago, if someone waved a patent – strike that, a patent application - in front of a venture capitalist, he or she would probably have written a cheque for an interest in the new company. Today, smart bankers are asking questions about claims, prior art, and competitive patent terrain. Some are even funding receivables from patent damages awards. Others are modeling the cash flow from patent royalties for potential securitisations. These days, financial analysts covering pharmaceutical companies obsess over patent expirations and FTC pronouncements that can dramatically impact stock prices. In a few short years, IP investors will find it increasingly difficult to get by without at least a modicum of patent literacy.

Best practices are beginning to emerge. Savvy shareholders are starting to view suspiciously mishandling of fiduciary obligations associated with IP. In the US, Financial Accounting Standards Board (FASB) rules 141 and 142 have forced managements and, in turn, institutional investors, to focus on intangibles such as patents and other proprietary rights. Starting in 2002, the FASB began requiring companies that acquire intangible assets to write them down within 12 months should they fail to meet certain impairment tests. This is a wake-up call for managements to get a handle on all their IP whether or not it plays a role in transactions. Previously, non-performing intangibles were swept into goodwill and amortised over a period of years, sometimes decades. Such strategies will no longer be easily justified.

In future IP Investor columns, I plan to discuss those who have learned how to secure significant returns from IP assets. People who talk about IP can be found at almost every conference and courthouse, but those who truly understand what IP assets mean and how to deploy them are few and far between. They include business speculators, licensing executives, technology transfer experts, patent litigators, valuation specialists, and even independent inventors. For the most part, lead players in IP success stories prefer to remain out of the limelight. However, in spite of their low profile, many are emerging as among the leaders of the knowledge economy.

The fact is that IP assets are not that different from real estate. While the market for patent rights is illiquid, transactions rarely transparent, and valuations difficult to calculate, patents are embedded in the economic foundation of what most developed nations now produce. In the Harvard Business Review (January 2000), Kevin Rivette and David Kline estimate worldwide licensing royalties at $120 billion. IBM earned about $1.7 billion from royalties in 2002, about $500 million of which were from patents. Profit margins on patent licensing are well over 90%. Qualcomm generated about $750 million over the same period and plans to do little if any manufacturing. Its business model relies on the high-margin profits generated from patent royalties. Manufacturing products derived from new technology is a risky proposition. By the time a plant gets built and put on line, a couple of years and billions of dollars are likely to have been expended. Without sufficient ROI, it may be a bigger risk not to seek patent royalties than to rely on the protection of what appear to be defensive patents.

Former Microsoft Chief Technology Officer and ThinkFire Services Chairman, Nathan Mhyrvold calls the exclusivity afforded patents "the illusion of exclusion". Indeed, for Mhyrvold there are few "Rembrandts" in the attic. Mostly, there are moths. The so-called patent masterpieces are where most people think they are: in the museum (or the homes of the wealthy). The real mystery is which patent strategies extract maximum value and help companies fulfill their shareholder obligations?

Future installments of IP Investor will explore the expanding role of investors, managers and advisors in securing IP returns.

Watching the overseers

2003

The failures of companies like Enron and MCI have put the actions, and inactions, of managements under closer scrutiny. But despite all of the attention being paid to tangibles, intangible assets, such as patents - perhaps the area of more significant mismanagement - seem to be escaping any scrutiny at all.

Despite their intense specificity, patents also are strangely amorphous. That for 95% or more of the time they have little or no value still surprises many. Is the exploding interest in innovation and intellectual property as important as it would seem, or are we really attempting to discern value that is too elusive to document or monetise? Who is best suited to standardise the accounting of intangible assets like patents? How reliable are current reporting methods? While the fall of Enron was not the result of poorly managed intellectual property rights, its fate was tied directly to inadequate oversight and unreliable systems.

A roundtable co-sponsored by the International Intellectual Property Institute and the United States Patent & Trademark Office was held last summer to bring to the public a candid discussion by IP thought-leaders about what impacts patent value. I was asked to organise it and moderate.

Frequently discussed; seldom understood

While many feel the economic impact of patents and other IP rights are the keys to global prosperity, others believe that the value of most patents, because of their nature, cannot be accurately determined. So, why bother? A small but vocal minority believes patents are anti-competitive and serve largely to enhance corporate wealth at the expense of innovation.

For corporate and financial managers, intangible assets represent a particular challenge. Just what do executives need to know to run their companies effectively and for investors to understand their performance? There is no simple answer. For those whose companies own IP assets that have been improperly exploited, there is trouble ahead; for those who don't have the assets to exploit, adversity also is likely. The point is that management is uninformed about what it is and doesn't have – the same essential lack of awareness that got companies like Enron and MCI into hot water. There is a reasonable likelihood that some companies are already hurtling towards intangibles problems, if not disaster. The problem is that we have yet to develop the tools or systems to discern it.

Diverse IP perspectives

The New Emphasis on Patent Value: Opportunities & Challenges Roundtable, held at the Cosmos Club in Washington, DC, brought together eight people from diverse backgrounds for a discussion about patents and how they are used in business. Participants included leaders from government, academia, business and law. It also included three former patent examiners, a United States Patent Commissioner, and heads of IP and licensing at companies large and small: – Dr. Margaret Mendenhall Blair (Prof. of Economics, Georgetown), Hon. Nicholas Godici (USPTO), Harry Gwinnell (Director of IP, Cargill), Dr. Joshua Lerner (Prof. of Finance, Harvard), James Malackowski (I|C|M|B Ocean Tomo), Marshall Phelps (Director of IP, Microsoft), Kevin Rivette (Boston Consulting Group). Hon. Bruce Lehman (IIPI) was a guest. I handled the moderating. (For a full transcript, visit: **www.iipi.org**).

The consensus of the group was that while innovation may be generating increased media attention, little effort has been made by those responsible for overseeing it to understand what it means to business performance or shareholder value. Most notably, intangible assets have received little or no scrutiny from senior management, financial management or Wall Street. It is unclear whether this is because of their apparent legal and technical complexity or because, except in certain companies – such as those in the pharmaceutical industry – patent performance is so difficult to quantify. What is clear to most of the New Emphasis group is despite the increasing importance of patents, management seldom understands its role in their ROI.

The roundtable discussion contains many anecdotes, insights and new ideas. Among the specific recommendations made by participants were:

- Reporting requirements should be necessary for all revenue associated with patents.
- Patent assignments should be enforced.
- Patent claims should be more readable. This could be accomplished by eliminating the "one sentence rule", which requires that a drafter's initial description of an invention be contained within a single sentence, no matter how long. "Let's use common English language construction so it is less difficult to read. So you don't need a patent attorney decoder ring and secret handshake to read the claims," said Kevin Rivette.
- The PTO should play a more active role in identifying standards for IP value. "I would suggest there is a great opportunity for the [US] Patent Office to spearhead, fund or facilitate a working group to deal with these issues," said one of the roundtable participants.

Managing corporate wealth

Standardising patent disclosure and discerning the meaning of patents to corporate performance and market valuation is no easy task. However, without attempting to do so, misjudgments will be compounded. Enron involved few if any patents. Still, the lessons it provides about understanding and overseeing drivers of corporate wealth speak volumes to the IP issue.

We can either brush this and other recent company failures aside as aberrations having little to do with proprietary rights, or we can challenge ourselves to come up with better systems for identifying, monitoring and conveying all assets, especially patents, before regulatory bodies require it. Without more consistent language to discuss IP and precise metrics to measure it, we are likely to spawn more lost opportunities than we have tools to discern.

The double standard

2003

Hold a property developer to ransom with a piece of land blocking a major building scheme and you are called a shrewd businessman. But demand a licence fee to use a patent covering key technology and you are branded a villain. Something's wrong.

Donald Trump is planning his next Manhattan skyscraper. He has acquired a suitable site on First Avenue, just south of the United Nations headquarters. A small parking lot, 20 feet wide, blocks access to an expanse of the proposed building's lobby. The lease on the lot does not expire until 2011. If Trump wishes to build his luxury tower soon he will have to purchase the land and acquire the lease at a hefty premium to the market.

In the above formulation, the astute parking lot owner is likely to be viewed as shrewd, a capitalist who through vision, luck or both, beat Donald at his own game. This person did not prevent progress; he merely made it a little more expensive for Trump, and possibly his tenants – prospective luxury condominium owners. Such is the cost of doing business in New York City. However, if an individual or company controlled an intangible asset, such as a patent, that required a royalty to be paid before allowing an optical switching system to be developed or a generic drug to be introduced, the cry would likely have been 'unfair competition'. The fact is that most IP exploiters tend to be seen as villains, and, occasionally, are regarded at patent terrorists. Real estate moguls, on the other hand, no matter how ruthless or profitable, are merely shrewd investors.

A double standard exists when it comes to exploiting intangible assets, especially patents. The impact on ROI can be palpable, and IP investors as a broad group, including companies, managers, researchers and shareholders, should be concerned.

All shoplifters will be prosecuted

Part of the difficulty is that IP assets – a combination of innovation, demand and legal rights – are abstract. The inventions they protect are often highly complex, and are not readily embodied. Rights violations are difficult to identify, expensive to document and arduous to litigate. To the untrained eye, valuable patents do not seem to be as deserving of the recognition afforded equally worthy hard assets. Compounding the problem is the proliferation of and access to digital products. Most law-abiding citizens believe that because good copies of digital content are easily made, they are there for the taking. If a teenager leaves a Virgin Megastore with the latest 50 Cent CD in his pocket and no sales receipt, he is shoplifting. If he accesses the same content from the internet, which he burns at home on his PC, or from a friend's previously purchased CD, he is exercising his rights under freedom of expression. Right.

It's amazing how many intelligent investors (Ben Graham, forgive me) and sophisticated, well-meaning executives still have difficulty taking intangibles seriously. To be fair, valuing IP is not an easy task. Even describing it can be a challenge. Unlike the equity, bond or real estate markets, most patents are illiquid, and transactions are seldom transparent. A common vocabulary for describing IP assets, strongly suggested by the US Securities and Exchange Commission and the Licensing Executives Society, has yet to be accepted. New US accounting rules adopted in 2001 require that intangibles included in an acquisition, such as IP, be valued and written down within one year if they fail to meet certain impairment tests. No longer can companies dump intangibles into goodwill, or allow them to languish for 20 years or more as part of an expensing schedule.

Facilitating progress

The limited exclusivity conferred on patents by government agencies such as the USPTO, EPO and JPO in return for disclosing the details of an invention is designed to stimulate innovation, not impede it. In general, patent systems have done an exceedingly good job achieving this. An inevitable by-product of more innovation rights, especially in a knowledge-centric economy, is a market for trading them.

A transparent market for IP rights not only facilitates demand, it encourages more accurate pricing and fuels investment in innovation.

Few patents, no greater than 3% to 5% by most accounts, have significant value. Even worse, not many people know what gives the good ones meaning. In many ways, speculating on IP rights is not very different from investing in real property. The difference is that a ready market for commercial or residential real estate helps to establish prices and stimulate demand. Most people "get it" when it comes to real estate. Few do when it comes to prime IP assets. Taking a financial position in an intangible asset, whether the owner plans to commercialise or otherwise exploit it, should not be viewed as an unnatural act.

Several years ago Ronald Katz, a Los Angeles businessman, acquired key telecom patents with no apparent intention of manufacturing products but every intention of achieving ROI. His 10-employee company generated some US $300 million in royalties in 2002 because others required his IP to do business. While this may have cost some companies and consumers, it also increased the value of certain technologies and products, and created a stronger market for related patents. In all likelihood, it increased shareholder value by hundreds of millions of dollars.

Katz is no more responsible for impeding progress than were speculators who purchased land in Kansas in the 1860s in anticipation of the transcontinental railroad. They were neither settlers nor railway owners, but businessmen who sought to buy land as cheaply as possible and then either lease it or re-sell it at a much higher rate. At first, the railroad companies were indignant about having to pay a toll to complete their route. In the end, cooler heads prevailed, and the roadblocks became building blocks for wealth on the new frontier.

Prickly profits

2004

Last month's IP Investor focused on the double standard applied to individuals and businesses that deploy intangibles like patents for profit, as opposed to investors who deal in hard assets. The net-net: real estate moguls are capitalists; aggressive exploiters of IP are anti-competitive. The following are insights from prominent patent owners, managers and advisers about the IP double standard and what can be done to mitigate it.

"By nature, people resist being controlled," says Harry Gwinnell, Associate General Counsel and Director of IP at Cargill, one of the largest privately owned companies in the US. "Everybody owns property, so they can identify with ownership of objects or things that can be touched. When it comes to intangibles, there is almost no base of experience. The USPTO is very clear that, in exchange for disclosure, a patentee is granted the right to exclude others. The inventor or assignee does not have to commercialise or even develop an invention to exercise his rights. Executives have difficulty accepting that a patent is merely the right to sue others to prevent them from practising an invention." Gwinnell is President-Elect of the Intellectual Property Owners, a leading association of IP holders.

Hon. Bruce A. Lehman, Commissioner of the USPTO, 1993-1998, is President of the International Intellectual Property Institute, a non-profit IP think-tank that seeks to educate governments, businesses and investors about innovation rights. "The confusion about IP is an absolute mystery to me," he says. "It's amazing how little is known about things that are so important. Economists often talk about patents as monopolies when the concept does not apply to patents but to businesses. As to those companies or individuals that may be blocked by certain patents, they are free to come up with a better solution. History shows that they often do. In many cases, a licence may be available. The recent European debate on software patents is a good example of how misguided most people are when it comes to patents. Many in Europe believe that software development will be brought to a halt as the result of permitting patents. In fact, the US was among the first nations to allow software patents, and it has 80% of the software companies in the world. Not everybody who owns real estate commercialises it. Nor should everybody who owns a patent be forced to bring a product to the marketplace. Demand for the right to practise an invention helps to validate it."

Not everybody agrees with Gwinnell and Lehman. Dan McCurdy is CEO of ThinkFire, Inc, a patent licensing firm that represents companies with large portfolios. McCurdy, former President of the licensing business of Lucent Technologies and an IP strategist at IBM, believes the patent system exists to encourage innovation and invention, not for the personal profit of individuals. "People like Lemmelson are conceptual inventors," he explains. "By tailoring their inventions to surround successful products they don't validate the system, they exploit it. They are doing nothing to advance technology, and are breaching the bargain the government provides to advance science in granting of the patent and allowing those who made the investment to profit in exchange for disclosing their invention. Innovation should not be something that speculators with no interest in technology or science can profit from."

Irv Rapapport has experience as an IP director, inventor and licensee. He was Chief Patent Counsel at National Semiconductor, Medtronic, Data General, Bally and Apple Computer. "Opinions on IP rights have more to do with the haves and the have–nots," he asserts. "When Cypress Semiconductor had no patents, T.J. Ross was going around telling everyone how evil they were. Once Cypress's patents started to issue the idea of having proprietary technology didn't look so bad. Patents can drive industries and stimulate competition. Most patents are pieces of paper, not worth what they're written on. Validating the economic value of an invention, no matter who is exploiting it or how it is being exploited, ultimately rewards the inventor."

"IP may be sold, bought, pledged and traded just like any other asset," says Dr Alexander Poltorak, CEO of General Patent Corporation, which represents independent inventors and smaller patent owners. "In economic terms, a patent is not really a monopoly but rather a public franchise. It is the single largest incentive for innovation. The patent system is inherently unfair to the small inventors. The right to exclude, i.e. to bring a legal action for patent infringement, does not come cheaply. With the average cost of patent litigation in the US in excess of US$2 million and as high as US$5 million the right to enforce is a theoretical concept of little value to many inventors."

Contrary to popular belief, says Poltorak, patents do not give the right to practise the patented invention. Instead, he explains, they provide the right to exclude others from practising the patented invention. "As far as the patent law is concerned, there is no difference between paper patents owned by an inventor (those that protect inventions that inventors do not practise themselves), and patents held by large corporations," Poltorak says. "Patents are nothing more than a licence to sue. Enabling small inventors to enforce their patents is the greatest incentive for all innovators. This inspires invention but also forces large companies with significant R&D commitments to pay attention to all patents and either license or design around them. Frequently, this leads to more and better innovation - the intention of the patent system in the first place."

Information is lacking about who most effectively exploits patents and how they do it. For my part, I believe that conferring value on patents supports innovation and prosperity. Patent assertions, despite the time, energy and expense they demand, help to validate inventions where they count most - in the marketplace. History shows that innovation's benefits are not always clear-cut. Conferring value on innovation, whether it is the result of exclusive commercialised products or patent royalties sought by warring parties, is integral to fostering scientific research and generating shareholder value.

Money grows on decision trees

2004

In many industries patent litigation is a fact of business life. It therefore needs to be treated as such by both company managements and investors.

The benefits of innovation are greater today than at any time in history. So are the costs. US patent applications doubled between 1990 and 2001; and have tripled since 1980. (EPO filings are up significantly, too.) Greater reliance on innovation rights to provide market exclusivity and generate income have also increased the investment risks associated R&D and enforcement.

While patent suits doubled in the US between 1991 and 2001, cases that go to trial remain steady at about 100 every year. As a result, a lower percentage of cases go to trial today (only about 3%). The increased focus on patent disputes in the business press conveys a somewhat distorted view of what typical IP dispute outcomes actually mean. Disputes over technology rights, especially patent litigation, can be more of an emotional response than they ought to be. The vast majority of patent settlements, in fact, are much smaller than those that garner headlines. For many companies, settling patent tussles is an inevitable cost of doing business, but one that managements and shareholders tend to see as a defeat.

This may be due in part to the failure of management and financial analysts to understand the economics of patent disputes.

Results, not headlines

At US$4 million to US$10 million or more for fees and costs in important cases in key cities, the cost of patent litigation in time, money and opportunity loss cannot be taken lightly. Even the deposition phase can run into the millions. Some believe that inevitable and costly patent conflicts are best resolved by business people who possess a sound awareness of legal and technical issues. The support of legal counsel, as well as damages experts, is essential. But counsel cannot make business decisions in a vacuum. IP investors should remain focused on the best possible result for their company and its resources over time, not on business headlines. Selecting the right combination of strategy and expertise necessary to resolve a patent dispute is as much their business call as their advisers' legal one.

When lawyers start talking to other lawyers, the scale, cost and time of a conflict often is ratcheted up. There are many times when attorney-orchestrated litigation is unavoidable, and the top patent litigators are, more than ever, worth their weight in damages assessments. But, as IBM has demonstrated repeatedly, securing the most favourable outcome is not always about being the toughest negotiator or blowing away infringers in court. Turning adversaries into revenue sources can mean more to a company's bottom line than standing victorious over their carcasses.

Patent disputes as business risk

Samson Vermont is a young patent attorney at Hunton & Williams in Washington DC who has devoted himself to analysing the risk data associated with patent disputes. He argues that because of the enormity of what is at stake - including sales, market share, damages, possible future licensing royalties, as well as the litigation costs - strategies for resolving patent disputes must be evaluated like other significant business investments. The fact is that they are not. Vermont says there is abundant and revealing data on patent disputes that most companies and their counsel seldom consider. Some confirm what we already know. However, a lot of the statistics are counter-intuitive and need to be incorporated into risk analyses, such as a decision tree analysis. Some of what Vermont's research reveals:

- At least 35% of patents that go to trial are found invalid.
- In 1991, 1,178 patent suits were filed in the US.
- In 2001, 2,438 patent suits were filed; of those only about 3% will go to trial.
- From 1983 to 1999, 76% of patent suits settled. The rest were tried, adjudicated, dismissed or transferred before trial. About 7% of the suits went to trial.
- The number of patent trials has remained fairly steady at 100 every year over the past decade, indicating that a smaller percentage of patent suits are going to trial than in the past.
- US patentees win about 68% of jury trials and 51% of bench trials.
- When infringers are first to file declaratory actions, patentees win only 38% of the time.
- About 63% of US patents lapse because of non-payment of maintenance fees.
- Approximately 1.5% of US patents issued to US companies are litigated.
- 0.25% of US patents issued to non-US companies are litigated.
- US patent holders of US patents are about five to six times more likely to sue for patent infringement than their foreign counterparts.

Informed investors

What does patent dispute analysis mean to IP investors? It means that management and other fiduciaries must not abdicate their role in accessing business risk when it comes to patent litigation. They need to avail themselves of relevant data and interpret it together with their advisers. It also means that factors such as the industry in which their company operates, technology and business objectives should be part of a bigger picture when allocating IP-related resources, including those for litigation. Knowledge of the predominant risk factors that determine ROI makes sense in almost every area of investment. Why should intellectual property disputes differ?

When winning can mean losing

2004

Obtaining the right decision in court does not guarantee a happy outcome for the victorious party. Because of this, companies need to be extremely careful before choosing full-scale patent litigation.

The decision to enforce patent rights is a complex one. Patent holders file suit for a variety of reasons, legal, financial and emotional. Companies frequently become involved in patent litigation for the wrong reasons or, at least, without knowing enough about the likely outcomes and how they may affect overall company objectives.

Patent settlements are not necessarily defeats. Companies that pay large sums for a licence to make a suit go away can come out ahead. Microsoft recently settled a three-year dispute with InterTrust involving patents on digital rights management technology for US$440 million. But, depending on how the licences were structured, the settlement is likely to yield billions of future profits for Microsoft. MS absolutely needs to be a player in the business of monitoring digital rights, especially those involving downloads. Unfortunately, not every company has $52 billion in cash reserves to settle disputes.

Because of the cost, time and pain of litigation, companies can win a case but not achieve a financial victory. This is why it is imperative that parties in a patent dispute have a firm handle on their objectives and risk data, which can help foretell outcomes. In the last IP Investor, we looked at patent dispute statistics, many of which are surprising. For instance, while the number of patent suits filed in the US over the past 10 years has more than doubled, the number of patent suits that go through trial has remained the same, and the trial percentage has shrunk to only about 3.5%.

"You can win a patent suit and still lose overall," says Samson Vermont, the leading purveyor of patent litigation data and a patent attorney in Hunton & Williams' Washington DC office. "Companies don't start large business projects without some analysis and forecasting, and they shouldn't enter into multimillion dollar patent suits without doing the same. The decision should be as much a business decision as a legal one."

Intangible costs

Since the median damages award in a US patent case is now only about US$2 million, companies that win a patent case can sometimes lose money overall because of the steep costs of litigation. For example, in a typical case, discovery alone often costs US$1 million or more per side. The entire cost through trial often exceeds US$2.5 million. Of course, patent litigation is not always about how much a plaintiff can collect in lost profits. Filing suit may have to do with intangibles, such as maintaining market exclusivity or securing licensees. It also conveys that a patent holder really means business and is prepared to make the necessary investments to defend its rights. But what Vermont is saying is that patentees should be more thoughtful about picking their battles. A careful economic analysis, including calculation of intangible costs, such as potential loss of shareholder value and customer reaction, should be considered before filing a patent suit. More than ever, disputes are a public forum. Companies that aggressively enforce against an alleged infringer need to focus not only on lost profits, but also on calculating likely returns.

Better forums for patentees

Jurisdictions mean a great deal in patent suits. For example, according to data reported by Professor Kimberly Moore of the George Mason School of Law, patentees have won approximately:
• 68% of the time in Northern California.
• 67% in Minnesota.
• 63% in the Central District of California, Southern District of New York and in the Southern District of Florida.
• 61% in New Jersey.
• 58% in the Eastern District of Virginia (the so-called "rocket" docket).
• 48% in the Northern District of Illinois.
• 46% in Delaware.
• 30% in Massachusetts.

The lesson of this data? Patentees should reconsider their habit of filing suit in Delaware. Patentees should not file suit in Massachusetts.

Time and venue

Between 1995 and 1999, the average time it took to resolve a patent dispute in the US, via settlement or otherwise, was 1.12 years. The fastest district over that period was the Eastern District of Virginia, at 0.43 years. The slowest district was the Western District of New York, at 1.97 years.

Unlisted companies or individual inventors are four times more likely to sue for infringement than large US companies. On the other hand, large companies traditionally tend to use their patents defensively. Their rationale includes minimizing various exposures from litigation, including damages and fees, to bad publicity are often influenced by a company's ability (or inability) to file counter claims on patents in a plaintiff's portfolio. This varies by industry. For example only about 0.5% of US chemical patents are litigated while roughly 2% - 3% of biotech patents are, with the incidence skewed toward the more commercially important patents. In fact, roughly one out of every four important biotech patents is litigated. An amazing figure, when you think about it.

According to Vermont, the chances of being sued vary greatly within a particular industry and area of art. Investors need to know that not only IP managers and patent counsel are well informed, but that senior managements and directors, too, are being properly advised. When it comes to patent disputes, there is no excuse for a weak handle on the costs of likely outcomes and alternatives.

Model behaviour

2004

In a few years the way in which patent disputes are conducted may change dramatically. If this does happen, it is not only rights owners who will be confronted by considerable challenges. Law firms and lawyers will have a lot to think about, too.

Intellectual property attorneys and law firms have benefited significantly from the worldwide boom in patents. Emphasis on turning innovation into value has fuelled competition to defend and otherwise monetise patents. But while IP lawyers are well equipped to administer patents, they may not always be in the best position to exploit them. As the business of IP has evolved, so have the economics of IP law.

Intangibles today comprise the bulk of the value of many companies. Between 1982 and 2002 the intangible assets as a percentage of S&P 500 market capitalisation grew from 38% to 85%. The changing emphasis has resulted in new ways of looking at both IP assets and the professionals and organisations that provide them with value. Managing IP is not a simple task; neither is identifying who is best equipped to do the job. There is no question that grounding in patent law, claim language and product-specific technology is essential. But what about IP market knowledge? What about the ability to price and deploy intangibles like balance sheet assets, such as real estate?

A provocative article by the editor and IP writer Mark Voorhees, "Ethereal Assets", which appeared in the 25th anniversary issue of The

American Lawyer, speculates about the role that IP law firms play in the IP value equation. "In the 1990s IP practitioners became 'alpha' lawyers by unlocking IP portfolio values," says Voorhees. "Now, can they become true entrepreneurs in the 'concept economy'?"

What hath law firms wrought?

Voorhees suggests at least three scenarios for IP lawyers, all of which potentially impact on IP stakeholders:

1. IP lawyers continue to be at the centre of IP monetisation, litigating big-ticket cases and engaging in major licensing transactions.
2. A variation on the first scenario still is positive for IP lawyers. Companies realise that IP assets are too important to be left in the hands of lawyers and assign them to patent-savvy business professionals who rely upon attorneys for assistance.
3. Here things get more complex. Voorhees suggests that law firms may decide to put their capital at risk the way investment banking firms do. Contingency billing, an occasional occurrence at the top law firms, could increase dramatically, as firms choose (or are required) to shoulder the increasing risk associated with patent litigation.

Well-organised non-law patent dispute firms – call them IP merchant banks – already have begun to establish themselves as viable alternatives to the costs and complexity of litigation. With experienced licensing experts talking directly to senior managers (not to lawyers) empowered to settle disputes, the emphasis is on business resolution. But resolving patent disputes, in or out of court, is a nasty business.

So compelling is this new but unproven model, some law firms with IP practices have established non-legal subsidiaries, such as Howrey Simon Arnold & White's Maxiam, formerly run by Roger May, past president of Ford Global Technologies, and Todd Dickinson, now chief IP counsel for GE. Foley & Lardner has toyed with the concept via INTX and even venerable IP firm Pennie & Edmonds, before it gently imploded, had established a patent licensing subsidiary. Well-established IP practices and firms have for some time quietly, and selectively, accepted contingency or mixed fee-contingency disputes. It remains to be seen whether senior managements at large companies are ready to enter into business partnerships that endeavour to turn disputes into business opportunities. Aligning various parties' interests can be a difficult matter.

Rainmakers and tribal chiefs

From my perspective, the shifting business model on which patent law firms and practices have been built provides insight into how IP assets are likely to be managed. Because of the increased frequency, cost and return on patent suits, partners who are adept at securing significant patent litigation work are at a greater premium than ever. The professional partnership is well on its way out at IP law firms, just as it was discarded by Wall Street in the 1980s. The few partners who control the flow of business – rainmakers if you will – are more powerful than ever. Supporting important but less essential service partners is clearly not their calling. To double and even triple their annual compensation, client-toting partners today need only walk across the street, as many already have.

Say what you will about the patent disputes, they help to quantify intangible assets, R&D spending and shareholder value. Because of the ever-expanding frequency, cost and pain of patent litigation, patents no longer can be the sole province of IP attorneys. With some traditional patent law firms at their apex, a few are sure to evolve into quasi-investment banks, where licensing commissions, transaction fees and return on well-placed capital are sure to outperform hourly billing.

What Voorhees does not say is that law firms, as we have known them, are optimally configured for patent litigation, not necessarily for maximising return on IP assets in less conventional ways. While complex disputes have made them more essential than ever, the cost and frequency of IP litigation also could price them out of business or, at least, thrust them into a new one. Patents now influence key business decisions that increasingly are coming under the scrutiny of senior management and shareholders. For now, patent litigators remain atop the IP food chain. Evolution may cause them to survive and prosper as they are, or to adapt to a changing environment. Time will tell.

Illegitimate assertions?

2004

The term patent trolling is frequently used pejoratively by IP owners that invest heavily in R&D to create their rights. But what, in fact, are IP asserters doing wrong?

----

patent troll (PAT.unt trohl) n. A company that purchases a patent, often from a bankrupt firm, and then sues another company by claiming that one of its products infringes on the purchased patent. — adj.
— patent trolling pp.

Patent trolls have been all over the news lately. The term has become synonymous with the unfair assertion of questionable IP rights and "extortion" of licensing royalties. Intel Corp coined the term a few years ago, when it was experiencing unprecedented attacks on its patents from financial speculators who neither produce nor practise inventions.

My interest in this month's IP Investor is not to knock owners who take advantage of weaknesses in the patent system or portfolios. I would rather explore the fine line between legitimate assertion of IP rights and those seeking a handful of royalty dollars through nuisance actions.

Fundamental to patent holders is the right to defend their rights by bringing suit. Companies with substantial patent portfolios are surprisingly vulnerable to challenge by small, independent patent owners who acquire rights for their strategic financial value. In this context, an independent's very lack of portfolio for a defendant to target in a counter suit becomes its strength. In the early days of independent patent enforcement, individuals or small companies seldom had the resources, or hubris, to challenge the patents of major companies. Notable exceptions were submariner Gerald Lemelson, intermittent windshield wiper magnate Robert Kearns and Eugene Lang, who founded Revco in the 1950s.

These people saw that the weaknesses inherent in the patent system regarding pendency and validity could be exploited. They also saw how vulnerable many large companies' portfolios are and how, in most cases, it made business sense for them to settle rather than litigate. Finding expert IP counsel to take their case was no easy task. Certainly, major law firms did not wish to support them against what could be potential clients. And while it is still difficult to get a major IP law firm or practice to take on some patent assertion cases, well-funded independents today are finding it easier to get quality representation. These days, law firms are less fearful about representing smaller plaintiffs, provided they have strong patents and sufficient financial resources. Indeed, in the United States, the high cost and protracted timeline of litigation may be a greater threat to innovation and return on IP (ROIP) than any of the challenges facing the USPTO.

Word plays

The image of the patent troll has been likened to that of a highway robber waiting to accost an unsuspecting citizen. This portrayal is only partially accurate and serves more to demonise adversaries, much like plaintiffs in personal injury actions, than to help investors understand the real threat.

"The use of the word 'troll' in this phrase is a sly linguistic trick," says Paul McFedries, author of Word Spy, The Word Lover's Guide to Modern Culture (www.wordspy.com). "It contains the sense of the fishing activity in which a baited line is dragged through water, usually from the back of a slow moving boat."

So, continues McFedries, a patent troll is, officially, someone who [bottom] fishes around for unused patents but is also, unofficially, a low, inhuman creature who only uses those patents for litigious purposes.

Large patent holders tend to paint a deeply dark picture of those who acquire patents for enforcement purposes. The implication is that companies who commercialise their own inventions and have made substantial investments in R&D are more legitimate than those who simply purchase others' rights to generate financial returns. Only those who use rights to protect market share and ensure profitability should be able to collect damages.

The public has little trouble with real estate speculators who buy uninhabitable buildings for the valuable land. Apparently, however, acquiring and asserting the rights associated with paper inventions is akin to blackmail.

Early citation

In an article in The Recorder, a San Francisco legal weekly, the assistant general counsel at Intel Corp said that he spends much of his time fighting off claims of patent infringement by companies that have never made a semiconductor device. In 1999 alone, the claims topped US$15 billion. Intel hurls the epithet patent trolls at the companies that want it to pay up. "We were sued for libel for the use of the term 'patent extortionists' so I came up with 'patent trolls'," the Intel attorney said.

I can see why independent assertion would infuriate patent portfolio owners. It plays on the inability of the system to issue fully qualified and thoroughly searched patents and the vulnerability of even strong, well-invested patentees. However, the last time I looked, doing business in a market based system means that all asset holders have equal right to maximum value, even if some have acquired a strategic advantage.

Patent quality costs

The National Academy of Sciences is calling for more funding for the USPTO where 3,000 examiners handle 350,000 applications a year with an average of 17 to 25 hours to check on the validity of a patent application.

Businesses claim a lack of due diligence at this stage often results in many patents being granted that should not see the light of day. (I would certainly not expect to find any patents of this nature in Intel's vast portfolio...).

Studies show that half of all issued US patents should not have been approved, and that the USPTO green-lights over 95% of all original patent applications.

Patent quality must improve. However, it is naïve to think that this alone will solve all of the ills of an eternally overburdened but inherently reliable patent system. Patent holders, regardless of size, financial commitment or commercialisation strategy, have the right to prevent unauthorised use of their inventions. Unfortunately, regarding patents as financial assets is a more difficult concept for some than others.

Buy low, sell higher

2005

Rather than complain about so-called patent trolls companies would be better advised to wake up to the reality of the patent system and use it to maximise corporate value.

"These [patent trolls] are lawyers and investors who buy cheaply or assume control over paper patents, mistakenly granted largely to failed companies," David Simon, Intel's chief patent counsel told BBC News recently.

Simon cites one case where a patent troll claimed a patent they had bought for about US$50,000 was infringed by all of Intel's microprocessors from the Pentium II onwards and that they were seeking US$7 billion in damages. In the end, the case was thrown out by the court, but it still cost Intel US$3million to fight, Simon says.

"The only thing the trolls have to lose is their patent," which, Simon says, "typically they have a very low investment in."

Easier said than done

To fund serious enforcement activity, independent plaintiffs need to conduct intensive technical, market and legal due diligence, replete with claims charts. They need to secure a financial partner and a good law firm, and convey to a defendant that they are in for the long haul and will not fold. They may have to wait years to see even a small return. This is not an easy way to make money, and players tend to be serious and knowledgeable about the IP in question. Inventors seldom have the funds necessary to identify or enforce infringement on their inventions.

Trolls are more likely to send out infringement letters, sometimes thousands of them, and wait to see what sticks. Defending them does not interest me. What does is the whining of companies with substantial portfolios who feel there should be a double standard regarding rights ownership: patentees who practise or commercialise an invention have the right to defend as well as profit from it; patent holders who otherwise acquire and deploy their rights do not.

Apparently, Intel asserting its IP rights against AMD or TI is legitimate enforcement; a speculator taking action against Intel is not.

Counterproductive, wasteful, distracting, even painful, nuisance patent suits are a product of imprecise grants and overburdened, under-trained examiners. Still, even 100 US$100,000 settlements are barely a dot on many companies' balance sheets. It's hard to believe that this should be driving costs up as to impact consumers and thwart innovation.

eBay, too, has come to think of the patent trolls as "an unfortunate cost of doing business", says the company's litigation and intellectual property professional, deputy general counsel Jay Monahan. "It's driven eBay's costs up and it diverts time and resources from building the world's greatest ecommerce platform [sic]. There are dollars spent on lawyers," he says. "There's also an impact on diverting in-house legal staff, engineers, people at all levels to produce documents and sit for depositions. Our approach to this point has been to vigorously defend ourselves against these claims and not to pay ransom money, if you will."

Hmm. Sounds like eBay is refusing to negotiate with "terrorists". Perhaps the company's patent portfolio is more vulnerable than it may at first appear?

It would be shameful if management refused to enforce the company's patents, on principle. As an eBay shareholder, I would be more concerned about ROI than finger pointing. Failure to collect patent damages or to generate licensing royalties on the company's infringed inventions would be a costly and embarrassing lesson in financial dynamics.

Responsible IP management

It's not at all easy to determine where patent trolling ends and responsible IP management begins. But it's a question that ought to keep senior management and their IP advisers up at night. Corporate officers and directors have a fiduciary responsibility to manage assets for maximum shareholder value – that is, to act strategically to exact a return on innovation. This means that if they possess – through internal development, assignment, acquisition or otherwise – patent rights that can be deployed for ROI, they must do so. Often, this mandate goes unfulfilled. The somewhat puritanical notion that there are acceptable and unacceptable ways of making innovation pay speaks more to a lack of understanding of IP market dynamics than to higher ethics. In the early 1990s, Texas Instruments busted open this myth with a series of aggressive and lucrative patent assertions.

Perhaps more dangerous than trolls is validating the notion that it is wrong to use patents and knowledge of the patent system for financial gain. Companies employ tax strategies to the benefit of shareholders, so why not patent strategies? It's difficult to condone the deployment of patents that should have not been issued or are taking too long to issue. However, they exist in every patentee's portfolio and we have various levels of dispute resolution to sort things out. The last time I looked, it is still not a crime to buy low and sell higher.

Patent enforcement is a high-stakes poker game. Sometimes it costs money to call a bluff. The inequities of the patent office are applied democratically. No matter how they are acquired, enforced or otherwise monetised, the same rights exist for all patent owners, regardless of their business strategy or capital investment. Some patent holders, however, are better prepared to profit from companies' weaknesses than others. Similar to First Amendment and free-trade rights, it is potentially dangerous to apply patent protections selectively. Assuring primary and secondary IP owners their due, while painful for some, typically leads to higher asset values for all.

No more name-calling, please

2005

Large patent portfolios fall victim to patents suits from small, independent asserters not because such people are "extortionists", but because the products they target are not as unique as their owners would like to believe.

The IP community needs to get a life. The term patent troll serves no one. Terrorist is even worse. Used to describe assignees that do not practise, but hope to profit from the rights to an invention, it underscores fundamental weaknesses in many companies. This is more than semantics. It's about an evolving understanding of innovation. Crying the "t" word over disputed patents threatens us all.

Some who assert patents could be considered extortionists. However, those with dubious patents out for the short money from businesses with deep pockets are relatively uncommon. Most of the speculators I run into conduct extensive due diligence others may have failed to. Their goal is to identify significant holes in a company's patent defence and to extract a return. Some have purchased rights from inventors who cannot afford to enforce them.

Most are willing to put their money where their accusations are. This newfound perseverance scares the heck out of companies that are not used to having their freedom to operate challenged by relative small fry. Patent assertion illustrates that, despite the R&D dollars that underlie many of them, large IP portfolios are often weaker than they appear.

Demonising asserters adds to the confusion. It makes it more difficult for CEOs, board members and others to distinguish between legitimately strong patents and weak ones, as well as shakedown artists out for a quick buck from those that can inflict real damage. The business media, the ill-informed, fans the flames of these misunderstandings. The result is that most company managements are reluctant to use their IP assets for greater profitability if it involves enforcing them. Fear of being branded a troll is a kind of 21st century scarlet letter. Shareholder value, be damned.

Independent asserters

Independent asserters is a more accurate term for those who choose to defend their innovation rights against infringers by entering into a licensing agreement or, if necessary, filing a lawsuit. Thoughtful IP owners are advised to refrain from labels that could be used to describe their own best practices. There is no prohibition against owning or enforcing patent rights without practising them. Succeeding at innovation may require that portfolio owners think more like their attackers, rather than hurl epithets at them.

Some companies seem to be taking a page from the independents' handbook. Hewlett Packard, Sony and Microsoft, for example, already are investing hundreds of millions of dollars in a patent acquisition fund. What they plan to do with these patents is unclear. Some companies are even segregating IP assets in a special purpose entity (SPE) remote from easy counter-assertion.

Innovation is the developed world's greatest business asset. While companies need more reliable, better-searched and timelier patents, they also need better mechanisms for resolving disputes. The greatest threat to innovation is the one-two punch of dubious patents and costly litigation. It should not cost US$4 million to US$10 million, nor take two or more years to prove a patent valid or not. Patent disputes are inevitable. How they get resolved is not.

Many of the large patentees who protest loudest ultimately rely on PTO inefficiencies to build, defend and profit from their own patent portfolios. It would be terrific if the USPTO (and the EPO and JPO) issued more reliable patents that could not be so readily invalidated (the rate is about one in three). But, because of high costs and difficulty retaining experienced examiners, that change is not likely to occur any time soon. Traditional patent litigation may not be the solution, but neither are unrealistic expectations about improving quality and making independent asserters go away.

Companies started the IP wars in the 1980s with significant resources – large patent portfolios and huge litigation war chests and the patience to dig in for the long haul. At that time, few inventors and businesses had sufficient means to defend themselves. There was little to fear. But the tables have turned. Today, well-informed and funded patent acquisition entities, and even law firms, are prepared to challenge the complex rights that protect inventions. The take-away: large patent portfolios are not necessarily comprised of good patents.

Potential backlash

Like nuclear powers, patentees with significant portfolios are armed to defend themselves against their peers. Many cases are settled with gentlemanly cross-licences. However, in a guerrilla war, the kind independent owners are likely to wage, Goliaths are often more vulnerable than Davids. Companies do themselves a disservice by grumbling about the inherent unfairness of the patent system, which they themselves help to perpetuate. They need to learn how to fight back with stronger, better-researched patents, smarter enforcement strategies, and more prudent approaches to licensing and dispute resolution.

Granting patent rights and establishing their value as intangible assets have a generally positive long-term effect on innovation and shareholder value. IP holders' reluctance to manage their IP actively, for fear that doing so is unfashionable or, even worse, unethical, may come to haunt them.

Companies and financial journalists must learn to distinguish between different types of patents assertions and not prejudge them based on who owns the rights or practises the IP. They also should be less arrogant about the ubiquity of their portfolios, despite their bulk or cost. Some companies' patents are more questionable than they are willing to admit. Independent asserters are in a better position than ever to prove it.

Patent rights... and wrongs

2005

A recently published book by two Massachusetts economists makes a notable contribution to the debate about the future of the patent system in the US. But not all the authors' conclusions stand up to scrutiny.

Engineering ideas to provide solutions and create value is as much the province of informed researchers as it is of lawyers and bankers. *Innovation and Its Discontents,* subtitled, "How Our Broken Patent System Is Endangering Innovation and Progress", a slim, engaging book by two Massachusetts economists, Adam Jaffe and Josh Lerner, has stirred up its fair share of controversy. The book provides a timely perspective about the inner workings of the US patent system and how the USPTO has fallen into disrepair. Researchers, investors and attorneys alike will benefit from the authors' rich historical insights, as well as from their recommendations for improving the system, which they believe impedes prosperity.

Where this book falls short is in its contention that US patents have reached a point of diminishing returns. Jaffe and Lerner argue that by allowing overly broad and "obvious" patents, the USPTO and the courts are a veritable monkey wrench in the machinery of American progress.

The authors point out that despite these beliefs and their academic standing (Brandeis and Harvard Business School), they are not "anti-patent" but anti "bad" patent. New areas particularly susceptible to poor patent quality include business methods, software and biotechnology.

Hastily issued patents are a problem when disputes arise. Proving an asserter's bad patent invalid can be costly and frustrating. But enforcing a valid patent is a legitimate and healthy exercise of rights that helps to confer value and keep companies on the straight and narrow. Without enforcement, profitability, shareholder value and innovation would suffer, and if there were no challenges, useful patents would be even scarcer (2% is the current estimate).

Perfect storm

At the root of the problem, say Jaffe and Lerner, is the CAFC, the Court of Appeals for the Federal Circuit. Established in 1982 primarily to hear patent appeals on decisions handed down by courts across the US and to provide more consistent verdicts, the Court's interpretation of patent law has not only made patents easier to obtain, but "easier to enforce against others, easier to get large financial awards, and... harder for those accused of infringing patents to challenge the patents' validity". In the years preceding the establishment of the CAFC, compulsory patent licensing made it undesirable for many companies to file them. The authors believe that a perfect storm, buffeted by strong patent holder rights, USPTO under-staffing, explosive technology growth and robust capital markets, has triggered an "overcorrection".

Patent troll is the term sometimes used to refer to a plaintiff looking for a quick settlement knowing full well that its patents are unlikely to be upheld. Trolls hope to obtain settlements below the cost of the legal action necessary to expose them, often US$1 million, or more. Jaffe and Lerner fail to distinguish between these dubious owners who coerce companies with deep pockets into throwing in the towel, and the majority of legitimate asserters, large and small, who have a duty to shareholders to generate IP value.

Innovation and Its Discontents is recommended for its take on patent history, as well as for opening the lid on legal strategies that position patents for ROI. The authors' suggestions for improving quality are reasonable and practical. They include the introduction of a more effective re-examination or post-grant opposition procedure to knock out patents that should have never been issued, diverting fewer PTO fees and hiring and retaining more examiners.

But Jaffe and Lerner miss the mark when they send out a distress signal that the broken system, tipped in favour of patent holders, rights, is stifling innovation. Come on, now. The US maintains the strongest patent protection for software. Surely, many patents issued to well-known companies would under scrutiny be found invalid. Still, the US software industry is by all standards the most robust in the world. Businesses of all sizes, as well as independent inventors, have not been deterred from filing software patents, despite the almost four-year period they take to issue. Erring on the side of the inventor facilitates far more innovation than it might quell.

No confidence

The authors believe that expanded patentability in biotechnology is of serious concern. "The granting of overly broad patents [such as on the human genome] that appear obvious in light of previous developments, and which grant broad rights that seem to cover with one patent many diverse possible uses", creates significant problems. Jaffe and Lerner are not wrong, but they have no confidence in the ability of the legal system and markets to self-correct and resolve most disputes equitably.

Poor patents are a serious problem. But narrowing their scope can only provide so much relief. Even with the proper resources, it is difficult for examiners to anticipate potential disputes, or how new technologies will evolve. Software and biotechnology inventions, in particular, have an ambiguous relationship to the products that they may one day protect. *Innovation and Its Discontents,* a more substantial primer than a polemic, provides a thoughtful context for anyone affected by IP rights or engaged in creating them, recommendations for saving innovation aside.

From the brink to the bank

2005

For a variety of owners, selling patents is considered off limits. Some, however, are beginning to take a more pragmatic view and they are finding a growing number of willing buyers.

Are IP rights the new commercial paper? That is what a prominent Washington patent attorney suggested to me recently. Patents are now being used to capitalise acquisitions, as well as to defray the costs of licensing programmes, R&D activities, filing fees and legal work. Buying or selling rights to uncommercialised inventions is emerging as a surprisingly effective method of strengthening a portfolio and supporting business goals.

Some believe that patent transactions are overlooked arrows in a patent owner's quiver. In the interest of full disclosure, for a little over two years Brody Berman has been acting as an agent to a handful of patent buyers and sellers. Patent brokerage is not something that we pursue; it seeks us. It started when interested patent owners, usually directors of IP or licensing executives, began coming to us informally asking if we knew where they might acquire certain types of patents. What interests them more than anything is discretion.

For those willing to discuss their objectives, acquisitions are primarily to shore up their portfolio for defensive purposes. The sell side is a lot simpler: these owners are looking to extract cash from patents they are not using, are not likely to need and, in many cases, have already sunk significant funds into. They are becoming less shy about using rights to capitalise business activities. Occasionally, it is to build a war chest for a licensing programme. I am continually surprised at the number and diversity of parties who want to acquire patents, including those in private equity. If our experience is any indication, the connotation of failure once associated with divesting or acquiring patents appears to be waning.

Patent buyers

A few companies have been active purchasers of patents for decades and have programmes in place to acquire them. Telecommunications and pharmaceutical companies are among the most active. Sometimes they buy direct from a seller or create an entity for the purpose of the acquisition. It is important to distinguish between those who want to take a licence from those interested in acquiring a small family of patents. Licensees typically desire the right to practise proven inventions; purchasers want patents for different reasons, which they usually are unwilling to discuss. It may or may not involve practising the patent.

A patent purchaser may be looking to shore up its portfolio for defensive purposes, or could be interested because it is preparing to launch a licensing programme or infringement suit and is concerned about counter assertions – that is, patents with some value, but which may no longer be relevant to the current owner. By aggregating patents – using acquired rights in conjunction with those they have previously acquired or plan to – smart portfolio owners can erect longer, stronger and less porous patent fences. Most buyers realise they can expect to see mostly B and C patents – that is, patents with value to some, but that may be worthless to the current owner. Few owners would put their A or core patents on the market, and most buyers would not want to pay the premium for them. To borrow a term from finance, there is an arbitrage in skillfully acquiring, repackaging and deploying IP rights with an eye towards their greater value. In a few cases, speculators are able to resell or flip purchased patents quickly at a substantial profit because they know who needs them. Sounds like the Manhattan real estate market to me.

Who are the sellers?

Sellers can be patent owners of any size or type, including universities, creditors' committees in bankruptcies and independent inventors. Traditionally, no one wanted someone else's cast-off rights to what were (and often still are) considered failed inventions. Bigger companies tended to view selling patents as foolish because of their vast potential, and feared that those sold could come back to haunt them in the form of assertions against their customers or cross-licensing partners, or, even worse, by patent trolls. (Many buyers will provide sellers and their clients with a licence to practise, but may not indemnify a seller's customers on patents they do not practise.) Smaller companies or independent inventors, for example, can realise fast cash from selling a small family of patents. US$1 million or more is not uncommon for as few as six of the right rights. On occasion, patent applications may be marketable at a small premium to filing and prosecution costs.

Patents are expensive to obtain and maintain, and especially costly to enforce. In addition to the R&D, filing and prosecution fees, there are translations, foreign filings and maintenance fees. These are, of course, negligible if the patent is associated with a successful, commercialised invention. However, how many patents are successful? According to industry experts, fewer than 5%, and as little as 1%, of most IT companies' patent portfolios have value. They are not just talking about royalty-producing patents but also strategic ones that protect market share or profit margins.

With this in mind perhaps 45% of a company's portfolio is probably necessary to maintain for defensive purposes or for possible future products. That leaves about 50% of most portfolios with orphan or unrelated patents (the figure may be somewhat lower in certain industries). The cost to maintain those unrelated patents, not counting the R&D associated with them, could be in the tens of millions of dollars. Triaging those patents certainly would save money, but selling a few of them before they lapse, even at low market rates, would generate several millions of dollars, with no downside risk (FACT: approximately two out of every three US patents lapse because of failure to pay maintenance fees).

Are CFOs and boards of directors faithfully representing shareholders' interests when it comes to managing patents for profits, or is their refusal to sell an emotional response to issues they do not fully understand? One wonders.

Dangerous conceits

2005

There are a number of reasons, many of which have little to do with hard-nosed business principles, why letting go of a patent can be difficult. But if companies are to do justice to their shareholders, they must take the sentimentality out of portfolio management "He called it Sleet's crows-nest, in honor of himself; he being the original inventor and patentee, and free of all the ridiculous false delicacy, and holding that if we call our own children after our own names (we fathers being the original inventors and patentees), so likewise should be denominate after ourselves any other apparatus we may beget."

Herman Melville, 1851

We see ourselves in our offspring. Like most parents, we observe in them an innocent future without limitation or flaw. Inventors and patentees, too, "free of all the ridiculous false delicacy", imbue their creations with the full weight of their hopes and dreams. While imagination is the fuel of innovation, when it comes to considering IP rights it is the seed of confusion.

Seeing patents for what they are (and are not) is a profound challenge. It is no easy task for an owner or inventor to prioritise a portfolio – to determine which rights are primary, which are non-essential but necessary, and which are better abandoned than maintained. Poor perspective afflicts small and large companies alike: corporate R&D departments and garage inventors.

Most would rather pay a small fortune in worldwide filing fees and legal costs until patents expire rather than make a decision to kill, transfer or sell them. It feels safer to hold on to all of something about which you are uncertain rather than take responsibility for the decision to manage it. The thought that someday a patent might be worth something to someone under certain conditions (it is, in fact, 100% of something) is provocative and difficult to contain. In the real world, however, holding patents is often more costly than folding them.

What harm is there in ogling our offspring? Melville suggests we drop the pretence about our creations made in our own image and simply call them after ourselves. The great novelist, who depicted Captain Ahab's vainglory in his blind pursuit of the white whale, similarly observed Captain Sleet's quest for perfection "in honour of himself".

Fixated on a windfall

Internet patent exchanges failed because they failed to discern how IP transactions occur. When it comes to licensing or otherwise transferring the rights to patents, discretion is the better part of valour. No owner wants competitors or customers to know it is acquiring or selling patents in a particular area and why. Even assignees can be difficult to discern, hidden by entities such as IP holding companies that are remote from taxes and counter assertions. I believe that's why companies, like the little one I run, have been drafted into the role of patent broker. If we make calls to the right people and a transaction ensues, needs are quietly served. If not, no one is the wiser. Advertising in *The New York Times* or on the internet, as if for a summer cottage, does not provide buyers a comfort level. Sellers, too, prefer that the marketplace not know what they are unloading, why and at what price.

Most innovators are fixated on a windfall from an industry-transforming invention sprung from the loins of their own R&D. Many companies, like those in the pharmaceutical industry, feel compelled to aim high or not at all. In some contexts, what are perceived as worthless rights protecting a stillborn invention are a resource worth aggregating. The notion of success and failure among patents (separate from an invention) is evolving, and grey is starting to supplant black and white. This is a relatively new concept. The huge number of invention rights that become unrelated to a company's business objectives, and which may no longer be the vessel of shareholder dreams they once were, need not be written off completely. To the right company at the right price and time, they may have meaning.

5-45-50

Only a small percentage of information technology patents support core products directly. The chart below was constructed with the help of a former Fortune 100 executive. It shows that a relatively small number of patents, perhaps 5%, are essential and perhaps another 45% are necessary or may be so. That leaves as much as half of a portfolio as unnecessary overhead, irrelevant to company objectives. Because jettisoning them could cause embarrassment, most companies pursue a scorched earth policy, allowing them to lapse with no benefit to the patentee or anyone else.

Anatomy of a patent portfolio

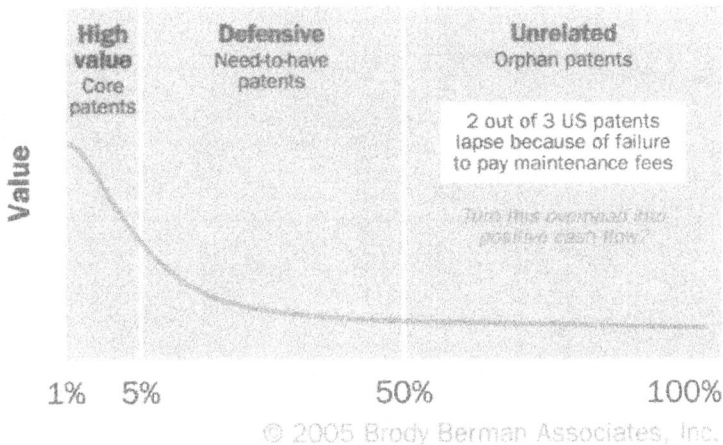

High value
Core patents

Defensive
Need-to-have patents

Unrelated
Orphan patents

2 out of 3 US patents lapse because of failure to pay maintenance fees

Turn this overhead into positive cash flow?

Value

1%   5%   50%   100%

© 2005 Brody Berman Associates, Inc.

Good news for sellers

The competition to buy patents is underway. This means that the market is becoming somewhat more efficient. Higher, more competitive pricing is on the horizon. Buying activity is still relatively modest compared to what it will be like in, say, five years. (For now, that's good news for buyers.) Demand has created a market for families of patents that are viable to some but that in the past had been destined for landfill. It is important to understand that all patent acquirers or aggregators are not merely trolls disguised as Robin Hoods; and sellers are not failed innovators.

Large portfolio owners are not necessarily more dispassionate than independent inventors about the relevance of their patents to their goals. The idea of a more perfect future, fear of failure and, perhaps, a little old-fashioned greed can colour what they see. Smitten with the notion of exclusivity, patentees forget that only on rare occasions do their rights have significant value, but that on many they may have some.

Little guys like him

2005

With a track record of generating multimillion-dollar awards for his clients, Ray Niro is not an attorney you want to be up against in a US patent litigation.

"I don't have to be liked by everyone, just respected," Ray Niro once told a reporter.

The founder of Chicago litigation boutique Niro Scavone Haller & Niro, he has developed a reputation for representing independent inventors and smaller companies in patent lawsuits in which he has an equity stake. To his adversaries he is often painted as a predator or troll, or, at least, as representing them. To his clients, he is a white knight.

Niro has been praised for giving independent inventors and small companies a voice and helping them level the playing field. In the high stakes poker game that is called patent litigation, spending US$10 million or more on a dispute that goes to trial is not uncommon. Needless to say, Niro – whose firm foots the bill for his time and costs – is selective about the cases he is willing to take on contingency. His team conducts a great deal of due diligence. He accepts fewer than 20% of the cases his firm reviews.

Track record

By any standard Niro's track record is impressive: more than US$500 million won in jury and bench trials and settlements in over 200 patent cases over 20 years. His best known cases include a US$57 million jury verdict in a trade secret suit against a snowmobile manufacturer and its engine supplier, which was later increased to US$75.5 million; a US$48 million jury award against an ink manufacturer; and a US$20 million patent infringement award against Square D Company. In 1997, the National Law Journal named him "one of the 10 best US litigators" and in 1999 it named him "one of the 10 best trial lawyers in Illinois".

Contingency wins, where he might share 40% or more of the recoveries, have made Niro a wealthy man. He lives most of the time in Boca Raton, Florida, and has a home in Aspen he built with former partner Gerald Hosier, who is best-known for generating more than US$1 billion in damages and royalties on behalf of inventor Jerome Lemelson, a known patent submariner until a 1996 change in the patent law to 20 years' exclusivity from filing effectively ended the loophole. (The Lemelson-MIT Program, endowed by the Lemelson Foundation, rewards unsung inventors. MIT describes Lemelson as "one of the world's most prolific inventors". The September 2005 decision of the Court of Appeals for the Federal Circuit that the Lemelson patents are not enforceable may mean that the Program's future income is more limited.)

Niro loves to go to trial. At 62, the admitted sports fanatic remains fighting fit, and lifts weights for 45 minutes, four times a week and cycles in Aspen's 8,000 foot altitude. He owns a Falcon 10 jet and at one time owned six Ferraris, including two 360 Spiders and a 575 Maranello. He has 10 grandchildren and has been married to the same woman for 41 years.

The son of an immigrant bricklayer from Abruzzi, Italy, Niro grew up in Pittsburgh where he says he learned to root for the underdog and still does. Trained as a chemical engineer, Niro retains that priceless ability to connect with juries and judges. "I learned early on that as a litigator you need to tell a story that juries and judges understand," he told me. "You can't talk down to anyone. I get great personal satisfaction from helping people to win cases which may not otherwise have been heard."

Frank Calabrese was an underdog. An inventor from Waynesboro, Pennsylvania, who claimed his invention – a patented data relay system – was stolen by Square D in the 1980s, sued when he discovered they had been marketing a similar system and refused to pay him for it.

Money doesn't matter

In the four years it took for the case to go to trial, Calabrese developed colon cancer. "Towards the end of the trial," says Niro, "Frank, who was dying, told me: 'The money doesn't matter. I want to be vindicated.'" And vindicated he was on 26th January 2000, when a jury awarded Calabrese US$13.2 million which the trial judge later increased to US$20 million. He died 19 days later. "Frank was grateful for what Ray Niro did for him," said Kathleen Calabrese, the inventor's widow.

"Ray was the only attorney we could find willing to take the case on contingency. And he worked hard and never gave up on Frank."

But not all of Niro's clients are defenceless weaklings. Some are investors like publicly traded Acacia Technology (NASDAQ: ACTG), which buys patents and asserts them because they understand companies' aversion to risk and low tolerance for the costs associated with complex patent litigation. To that Niro responds that while he prefers to work directly with inventors and small companies, middlemen can benefit the system and have the right to exist.

"When it comes to using patents for business advantage," concludes the bearded litigator, "the little guy is not the one who is gaming the system, although many defendants would like you to think so."

An American original

2006

The next time a call centre asks you to "select one for this, two for that or three for the other thing", think of Ron Katz. He is virtually everywhere.

Ron Katz has received surprisingly little recognition. His detractors – mainly infringers and their representatives – paint him as a troll, fishing around for a vulnerable company to sue. In fact, over a 40-year period Katz has identified, patented, practised and licensed dozens of inventions that scores of companies need in order to do business. If anyone qualifies as an American pioneer on the knowledge frontier, it is Katz. But don't expect to see him on the cover of TIME anytime soon.

The most financially successful inventor in history, Katz has generated revenues to date approaching US$1 billion in licensing fees on his call centre patents and expects to double that figure by 2009.

In 1961 Katz, 24, and partner Robert N Goldman formed publicly owned Telecredit, Inc, the US's first realtime credit and cheque cashing verification service. They were granted a US patent on the invention that underlay the company's products. When Telecredit hit some rough spots, Katz turned to licensing for additional revenue. "This was prior to the Federal Circuit Court of Appeals and patent owners were having difficulty prevailing in court," says Katz. "Pursuing reasonable settlements by offering fair terms was the only way to go."

Around 1985 Katz saw the potential of combining computers with telephones to achieve new forms of interactive processing. He is named on over 50 issued US patents covering systems relating to automated call centres, interactive voice response, credit verification, video monitoring, anti-counterfeit and merchandise verification.

"He has never studied engineering or computer science," observes Evan I Schwartz in his incisive profile on Katz in Juice: The Creative Fuel that Drives Today's World-Class Inventors (Harvard Business School Press), "and yet was the first to sketch out a critical set of new information technologies that the world would want and need, an achievement that has put many major corporations on the defensive." Studying back office transactions, such as voluminous cheque and phone call processing, and thinking about ways to improve them, are among Katz's interests. He enjoys identifying ways of making businesses more efficient and has helped to streamline processes or make them more reliable. Companies tend to take these improvements for granted and will pay for them only when they must. Schwarz notes that a visitor [to Katz's small office in Los Angeles] "sees no clutter, no gadgets, no machine tools, and no engineers at graphical workstations".

Katz helped to change how innovation is understood by regarding information processing as a series of inventions that can be enhanced, protected and made quantifiably more profitable.

"Companies will consider taking a licence when you show them the value," says Katz, who is proud of his record of never having gone to trial – although he has always been prepared to do so, if necessary. "Initial reactions can vary widely and they often need to be convinced it is in their own best interest to pay. Often, it's easier to get management to agree to pay a reasonable royalty rather than bury their head in the sand and risk a large cash verdict and even an injunction."

Katz emphasises that independent and large corporate inventors alike must have the goods to succeed: good invention, good patents that read on them and the resources and resolve to persevere in disputes with infringers.

Katz has guest-lectured on negotiations for 12 years at Stanford University's Graduate School of Business. Through Ronald A

Ron Katz, an IP pioneer

Katz Technology Licensing LP (RAKTL) and its affiliate, Katz has successfully negotiated more than 150 patent licences to such companies as IBM, Microsoft, AT&T, MCI, Delta Air Lines, Bank of America and Merck.

While the troll image may be an inaccurate depiction of him, the fishing one is not. Katz – whose older brother Joel Grey won an Oscar in 1972 for his role in Cabaret – likes to get away from it all by salmon fishing in remote areas of British Columbia. He also enjoys spending time with his six grandchildren in Hawaii where, he says, "I can walk on the beach, clear my head and come up with new ideas."

Despite his successes or, some speculate, because of them, a rare ex parte or USPTO Commissioner-requested re-examination of four of his call centre patents was initiated in 2005. If successful, it could impact some of Katz's future enforcement efforts. (He has 48 other interactive call processing patents fully intact.) If not, it is sure to reaffirm the value of his rights and ability to enforce them. Some believe that, under intense political pressure, the USPTO is succumbing, pre-emptively, to companies which fear that it is only a matter of time before they will have to take a Katz licence. But this is not stopping Katz. In July 2005, RAKTL filed a patent infringement suit for his call centre patents against Citigroup, Morgan Stanley's Discover Financial Services, T-Mobile USA and Wal-Mart Stores.

Note: As of 2013 RAKTL patents have generated an estimated $2 billion in licensing fees.

Skin deep

2006

A recent survey on patent quality in the United States poses more questions than it answers.

It's been said that beauty is in the eye of the beholder. So, too, it seems, is patent quality. Intellectual Property Owners (www.ipo.org), an association dedicated to the needs of patent and other IP owners, and populated by many of the most prominent ones, recently conducted an opinion survey of US patent quality. The results were surprising but inconclusive; an indication that perspectives vary as to how well patents provide certainty about who owns a US invention. Despite protestations in the press about trolls and other rights predators, about half of all US filers are pleased with the quality of patents being issued by the USPTO. Only 47.5% of respondents to the IP survey (89% of which generate more than US$1 billion in revenue) are less than satisfied, and 48.8% are satisfied or very satisfied.

Greater disparities occur, however, when taking into account the industry in which companies operate or their annual revenues. When asked "How do you rate the quality of patent being issued in the US today in your industry or field?" The results showed that not all large companies think alike.

Among computer, electronics and software (IT) companies responding, only 40% said they are less than satisfied with the current state of issued patents. However, 10% of the IT group – more than twice the number of the overall survey– consider patent quality in their industry poor. This is in marked contrast to the chemical, pharma and biotech area, where 54.5% were less than satisfied but not a single company reported quality in the poor range. And why not? Asserters with weak patents tend to prey on large IT companies with products on which several or more patents may read, and which do not want to risk an injunction or pay damages awards. Businesses with chemical or pharmaceutical products tend to be spared because invalidity is less of an issue, as oftentimes one patent covers a single successful product or compound.

Size matters; so does industry

The largest companies (US$50 billion or more in annual revenues) were far less satisfied than merely big companies (US$10 billion to US$50 billion) and smaller companies (less than US$1 billion). Those respondents in the smallest size group are the most positive, with a whopping 22.2% reporting they are "more than satisfied" with patent quality. The survey does not detail how many among the largest companies fall into IT, chem-pharma, and consumer-manufacturing categories. Perhaps it should have.

The questionnaire was sent to 139 companies, all of which were IPO corporate members and patent holders. Of those companies, 80 responded. Thirty companies were in the computer, electronics or software field. Twenty-two respondents were in the chemicals, pharmaceuticals or biotech field. Sixteen respondents were identified as consumer products, machinery, or general manufacturing. Twelve companies were in a field other than those listed.

Of the 80 companies that responded, 16 reported annual revenues exceeding US$50 billion, 29 reported annual revenues between US$10 billion and US$50 billion, 26 reported annual revenues between US$1 billion and US$10 billion, and nine reported revenues less than US$1 billion. Hence, 71 out of 80, or 89%, of the respondents, were from companies that generate more than US$1 billion in annual revenues. It would have been interesting to see differences in attitudes among companies in the lower end of the under US$1 billion spectrum, which rely on fewer patents for freedom to operate or raise capital and have less to lose in a possible counter-assertion.

Does size colour perception more than industry? To some extent, yes, depending upon the industry. Oddly, some large IT companies, disillusioned by uncertainty and long pendency, are suggesting an end to the patent arms race. They want to facilitate fewer, better examined patents that are less subject to dispute.

Computer, electronics or software

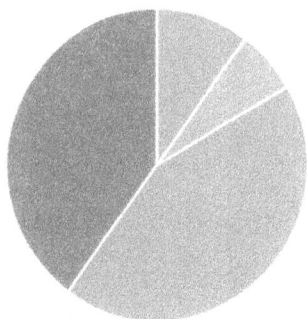

MORE THAN SATISFACTORY 6.7%
SATISFACTORY 43.3%
LESS THAN SATISFACTORY 40%
POOR 10%

Source: IPO, patent quality survey

Patents are more abundantly filed and quicker to issue in the IT industries than in chemical or pharma areas. Big pharma wants to hold onto injunctive relief that can potentially shut down an infringing generic. In the IT world, that same approach can cripple a successful electronic device company such as Black Berry maker Research in Motion (RIM). IT companies, thus, are more vulnerable to small companies, independent inventors or speculating trolls with dubious patents.

Are companies, especially IT companies, really helping the US and other PTOs to issue stronger, better researched patents that are less likely to be deployed unfairly? Is the legal system or are companies to blame for allowing inevitable disputes over inventions to become so costly to resolve? Perhaps a future survey will reveal more about this. For now, kudos to IPO for exploring how patent quality is as much a part of perspective as the law.

Patent quality is often confused with patent value. Some dubious patents are valuable, while many well-issued ones are not worth the paper they are written on. Quality and value are rarely synonymous, but for most businesses bringing them into closer synch means less uncertainty and greater return. Investors take note.

Patents don't kill innovation, people do

2006

Many believe that because patents are too readily obtained, the bad ones are gumming up the system and destroying innovation. They are wrong.

While broadly issued patents that should not have been granted are a drain on resources, they have a less significant impact on innovation than the growing length of pendency at patent offices around the world and the high cost of resolving disputes. It is not the patent offices' alone that are responsible for uncertainty. The arduous methods we have come to rely upon for resolving patent disputes and the filers themselves also play a role.

Among the patent system prognosticators are many otherwise sober business executives, economists and journalists who believe the system is on the road to Armageddon. This includes Reed Hundt, former FCC Commissioner under President Clinton, who recently wrote in *Forbes* that: "We should slash the number of patents granted each year by 90%. Most technology should not be patentable." In Innovation and its Discontents Adam Jaffe and Josh Lerner, professors of investment banking at Harvard Business School, say the system is severely broken and needs extensive repair.

The patent system may need to be improved, but it should not be scrapped because many of the patents granted in some arts eventually are found to be insufficiently novel. Innovation is a complex process. It is virtually impossible to tell which products will be important when patent applications are being examined. Thus, while many ideas are protected, only a handful are worthy. Uncertain patents undermine planning and make accurate valuation more difficult. They inhibit the formation of a marketplace enjoyed by other assets such as securities and real estate.

The real danger

Many patents are issued by the USPTO, EPO and JPO. Because examiners do not have anywhere near the resources – or the hindsight – of litigators, it is impossible for many patents to issue without a high degree of uncertainty. For some companies filing patents it is merely a numbers game which they know they can win; a thicket which makes it difficult to see the forest for the trees. But should it be the job of the major regional patent offices to examine applications for the various tests of nonobviousness and novelty, and be in the position to judge the sincerity of filers? If p0atents take too long to issue or do not issue properly because examiners are hampered by applicants, it is not the patent offices that are endangering innovation.

A growing backlog of patent applications must be taken seriously. In the USPTO the backlog is up to 400,000 patents and average pendency is about 2.5 years overall and more than four years in some arts. Unless the system is harmonised, by 2010 patents are expected take six years or more to issue, creating even greater uncertainty. In the USPTO, most filings –56% – are from non-US applicants (13 of the top 20 US patentees are foreign-based companies). In the EPO, 66% of applications come from non-Europeans. So this is far from a local problem.

The USPTO approves 95% of all original patent applications, compared to only 65% in Europe and Japan, wrote one IAM contributor recently.
"It is relatively easy to obtain patents with broad claims and questionable validity, leading to an increased number of patent lawsuits – currently

three times that number [filed] in the 1980s," they concluded. Are large, international filers merely flooding the system with broadly drafted junk, hoping to get lucky or gum it up? I do not think so. I have more respect for the business of innovation.

Uncertainty and cost

A lack of patent quality leads to greater uncertainty, which leads to higher costs, poor planning and less value. The USPTO cannot make much headway improving patent quality on its own. An end to fee diversion along with more and better trained examiners will help, but what patents need most is a more efficient marketplace, an apparatus for readily determining value that does not require constant, costly and painful intervention by the courts. They also need help from filers. Identifying prior art, especially non-patent prior art, is often like finding a needle in a haystack. The USPTO cannot do it alone.

The USPTO is a lot like the IRS. If a filer wants his or her accountant to engineer a tax return that results in a nice fat refund, it is not very difficult to do so. That does not mean that he will not be subjected to back taxes, fines, audits, jail time or otherwise punished for taking deductions that he is not entitled to. Similarly, it is not difficult to get a patent attorney or agent to get a patent to issue. Who cares that under the scrutiny of litigation or re-exam it may not hold water? It is unlikely the patent will ever get that far. Many consider it a calculated risk that a poorly examined, overly broad patent will not come back to bite them on the behind. And even if it does, chances are that in relative terms it will not cost much to settle the dispute.

Cynicism about the patent system weakens invention. The current method for vetting patents and identifying quality works, but is highly inefficient. Frequently, the more a patent is worth, the more arduous and costly the process to substantiate it. It is impossible in most arts to determine upon issuance whether a patent will stand up to the rigours of litigation, let alone the marketplace. Until recently, the inefficiency sat well with most large companies. Now, huge damages awards, the potential for injunctions from trolls and other potential dangers are causing some filers to rethink their notion of patent filing and ROI. Sometimes a bad patent is worse than no patent at all.

Like death and taxes

2006

It is not just patent offices that are responsible for the issuance of poor quality patents; filers have to take their share of blame as well. And until they do, things are unlikely to get much better.

The only thing certain about most patents is their uncertainty.

Don't let anybody tell you otherwise. Questionable, self-serving patent strategy has as much to do with quality, or the lack thereof, as do redundancy among the PTOs or damages awards. While patent offices need to do a better job, they cannot be blamed for all of innovation's ills. Filers have to shoulder their fair share of the blame.

The patent offices comprise a beleaguered system of government issuers who, like many agencies, are easily manipulated. Huge backlogs and unshared examinations and prior art searches do not help. However, some companies may finally be realising that taking advantage of the situation by getting bad patents to issue, or establishing an arms race in which few can compete, may be coming back to haunt them. Rising legal costs and, especially, damages awards are conspiring to make R&D more expensive and less productive, and planning next to impossible.

When it comes to innovation, a degree of uncertainty may be inevitable in some industries. A more practical approach to resolving disputes earlier might help. A hard line on the part of some parties exacerbates the situation. I understand that BlackBerry maker RIM could have settled its dispute with NTP in 2002 for less than US$50 million. Eventually, under pressure from the courts and distributors such as Sprint, a settlement was reached for US$612.5 million.

Did RIM really think that stoking popular opinion among BlackBerry users through the media or a protracted, politicised re-examination would win out in the end? Were I a RIM shareholder I would seriously consider a shareholder derivative suit for misunderstanding the courts and misreading the marketplace.

Haves and have-nots

That's the irony about costly patent settlements. Few companies want to be a licensee and pay millions for the right. But in the end it is a hell of lot cheaper to pay royalties than have a court order you to pay damages. Simply put: companies need to do a better job of understanding not just what they have in their patent portfolios, but what they do not have, and what it costs to get it.

There is a disconnect when it comes to patents and pricing. It does not take an economist to know that uncertainty causes mis-pricing, which in turn can create opportunities for smart, fast-moving value-seekers and havoc for businesses trying to plan. Burying one's head in the sand, as RIM has seemed to, does no one much good. It certainly is not what intelligent shareholders want. Moreover, it helped to give users a reason to consider and adopt other mobile messaging devices, such as those from Palm, Microsoft and H-P.

It's worthwhile to be reminded that 13 of the 20 largest US patentees are not US-based companies. What this means is that uncertainty is a world problem, and a very dangerous one. Many nations have a vested interest in reliable patents and more will in the future. The time to take an honest look at patent reliability is now. We need to understand why it impacts some industries more than others. We need to understand how we got here and how to fix a system beset with national politics and plethora of vested interests. This is a serious challenge. At the same time, addressing the reliability issue also presents extraordinary opportunity. Amidst the piles of patent rubbish is the future. We can all benefit by taking time to consider how innovation and financial markets can complement one another, and not just point selected fingers at PTOs, trolls or the patent bar.

It's unhealthy that the only certainty about patents is that most of them are unreliable. But it's ridiculous to think that the virus can be eradicated with a random dose of anti-biotic. Prior art searches must put more of the burden on filers and not just the patent office or those who seek to challenge validity in the courts. I'm not suggesting that we give up on improving the patent system or on achieving harmonisation among the world's PTOs. I am saying that when questionable patents become the norm, liquidity and pricing go out the window. Unenthusiastic prior art submissions should be held to as high a standard as poor PTO searches.

Trash talk

Even if RIM was an unwitting infringer, did it and thousands of other companies have the resources to conduct proactive prior art searches on their own and others' inventions that exceed PTO criteria? You bet they did. Companies choose not to for complex legal, business and social reasons, undermining patent quality in the process and defaming the system.

I support patent reform and harmonisation. But like changes in the tax code, I am afraid that it is only a small step on a very long journey. Reliable patents require cooperation. Companies that think they can talk about better issued patents and file gibberish may be mistaken. For too many, quality-speak is really trash talk.

Better patents require participation by filers as well as examiners. Companies cannot participate by cheering from the sidelines. Legislation on behalf of quality goes only so far. Filers in all patent classifications, not just software and business methods, need to act like they have a vested interest in facilitating reliable patents which can minimise disputes and help PTOs conduct the best possible searches. Currently, I'm uncertain many do.

Kicking and screaming?

2006

It remains to be seen whether patent owners will need to be dragged kicking and screaming into the 21st century.

Most patent portfolio owners fear patents being transacted like tangible assets. The reasons are complex, cultural as well as financial. But it is the lack of information about reliability and transaction specifics that they fear most.

Many companies still view patents as little more than necessary legal documents. However, developments such as patent auctions and other approaches that serve to mark-to-market worthwhile IP have caused some to view a lack of financial IP strategy as shortsighted. Informed shareholders already are putting pressure on managements to view strategic IP for the assets they are (and are not), and active IP management as a core business competency.

No other asset class rivals patents' lack of certainty and patent transactions' lack of what the financial markets call transparency. Further complicating matters are inconsistent rulings and high costs associated with patent infringement. Companies with significant product revenues cannot always tell when they will be slapped with a patent suit orinjunction. For many, patents as investments are a recipe for anxiety. But those who dare to squeeze more profit from the rights to practise inventions are a growing and increasingly vocal presence.

Sophisticated sportsmen

When it comes to deal scrutiny IP is where venture capital was maybe 30 years ago. Largely the preserve of a few wealthy investors-cum-sportsmen, such as the Whitneys and Rockefellers, transactions took place under the radar. Few cared to change it. Success of this asset class, accompanied by greater awareness, led to higher multiples for all. The genius of the early VCs was that rather than hide from scrutiny, they quietly embraced it. These investors, financial engineers in many ways, learned quickly that not only is limited self-disclosure more palatable than government regulation, it is also good business.

The impact was to create a comfortably unregulated market with disclosed pricing and structure. The inevitable demystifying of venture capital investing created more opportunities for different types of investors and more capital for emerging companies. Today, venture capital still is principally an unregulated industry. There are many types of venture investors and dozens of periodicals and newsletters that cover private equity and portfolio company performance. The news is surprisingly detailed about buyers, sellers, prices and terms. None of this disclosure is required.

Transparency is no guarantee of success. Venture investments still lead to far more failures than successes. But limited disclosure of IP licences, asset sales and financial transactions helps to make more accessible a complex and difficult asset class. It affirms that some assets clearly are more worthy than others, and that many are taking innovation rights as seriously as tangible corporate assets. It also allows investors to make better informed decisions. More information will not prevent investors from making mistakes, but it can provide the background for intelligent decision making.

Joseph R Flicek is managing director of Amphion Innovations plc (New York and London, LSE: AMP), which develops and finances innovative companies. He believes that understanding a company's intellectual property position is essential. "Public companies are required to convey great detail about the status of tangible assets that they develop or acquire," he says, "but little or nothing about what are often their most important assets, their IP. This can understate, or overstate, the real progress of a company and its value to investors."

Make markets, not war

Fewer than 3% of the patents in most high-tech portfolios have any value. Identifying which ones do is daunting. Short of patent litigation it is difficult to know what a valid patent or family of patents is worth at a given time. While litigation can help put a number on the table, it is painfully inefficient as a pricing mechanism.

"Compared with other assets classes, IP is more difficult for investors to value, but that doesn't mean it should not be," says Robert Kramer, managing partner of Altitude Capital Partners, a private investment fund that focuses on IP that recently closed a US$200 million round of financing. "IP transactions require more complex and costly due diligence and developments in the courts need to be interpreted for their financial impact."

Some say that IP transactions, by nature, cannot be too broadly disclosed; that anonymity and strategy go hand in hand. I don't buy that. As with venture deals, a lot of information can be shared without compromising competitive advantage. Doing so serves the interests of companies, shareholders and inventors alike.

Companies with significant IP holdings, which are confident about their value, should encourage others to bring on the competition. If they have the goods, it can only improve valuations. Companies that maintain stockpiles of patents that do not read on the right products run the risk of seeing their IP strategy tumble like a house of cards. Today, they can do something about it.

In increasing numbers, well-capitalised patent owners, by whatever name they are called, are refusing to cower before patent stacks that they believe may be flawed.

Portfolio owners should welcome this new found confidence in the emerging IP markets as a wakeup call – an opportunity to improve their position quietly and possibly avoid costly disputes.

Whether through public or private auction, or one-on-one trade, or through private equity investment, IP transactions are here to stay.
Most companies eventually will engage in them. IP asset transfers have the ability to enhance shareholder value, improve returns on R&D and foster innovation. For some they will be keys that unlock profits; for others they will reveal weaknesses they may not otherwise had been aware of.

Dumb and dumber

2006

Outlawing broad patents on unusual inventions is a bad idea. It is more likely to destroy innovation than fuel it.

There is a movement afoot advocating that stupid patents should not see the light of day. Proponents believe that this spares business and society the cost of ludicrous inventions. I think these watchdogs are the silly ones – a case of dumb and dumber.

"A Patent on Foolishness" typifies the how these misguided reformers see things. The article was published in July in *What We Now Know,* by Casey Research (www.caseyresearch.com), a publication that describes itself as "a bi-weekly newsletter for the investor-freethinker that keeps you in the loop on the economy, politics, health, science, technology, and more". It details some of the many colourful and apparently ludicrous patents that have been issued by the US and other patent offices, presumably at the behest of vain inventors and zealous attorneys.

"Have you ever used a laser pointer to drive your pet crazy?," the article asks. "You may soon have your day in court because you infringed on (US) Patent No 5443036, Method of Exercising a Cat, including 'any other animals with the chase instinct'. And if you, after reading this, think you had better go back to having your dog fetch a plain old stick, beware.

There's a patent for that, too. (No 6360693, Animal Toy.)… In Australia,

John Keogh, a freelance patent lawyer striving to expose the faulty system, managed in 2001 to patent a Circular Transportation Facilitation Device, aka the wheel… Patent laws were originally designed to protect truly innovative ideas from being stolen by others…"

The whole story

As evidence that the system is broken, the unnamed author cites the Electronic Frontier Foundation and Professors Lerner (Harvard) and Jaffe (Brandeis), co- authors of the misguided *Innovation and its Discontents*. (My review of this book, "Creative Thinking", can be found at www.brodyberman.com.) Says WWNK: "…All kinds of non-innovative items and simple methods have been granted patents, and litigation – often involving tens of millions of dollars – is going rampant. Some patents might indeed threaten not only the uninhibited development of new technologies but the very fabric of modern society."

Having a laugh at the expense of what appear to be outlandish patents may make for good copy, but it does not tell the whole story. My guess is that more large portfolio owners than independent inventors are filing ridiculous, system-clogging patents that should never have issued. Indeed, some of the most incredible ones may not be so outrageous after all. The idea of the "one-click" internet purchase decision promulgated by Amazon.com, while irksome to some, was eventually licensed to Apple in 2000. Some large filers would have you believe that it is everyone but they who are soiling the system. Good ideas that are readily accepted can appear to be generic. At some point, the alphabet was probably patentable: "Great idea. Why didn't I think of it first?" Actually, someone probably did. The problem was they failed to file on it in a timely manner and to raise the capital necessary to enforce their rights.

The patent system does not prohibit the use of an invention. It allows patent owners to prevent others from doing so. This is an important distinction. In the US, it is the district courts and CAFC which are responsible for understanding the practice of an invention. Until recently, few patentees had the resources to oppose infringers and many patentees were content to cross-license. Patent offices are in no position to judge what is important or "truly innovative". They should stick to the business of accessing patentability and leave relevance to the marketplace and, if necessary, the courts.

We live in a distinctly idea-driven economy. If the sanctity of an invention that meets the tests of patentability is not respected, no matter how absurd it may seem, innovation will suffer. Like free speech, the right to secure a limited period of exclusivity for an invention in exchange for disclosing it is the bedrock of a civilised society. Of course, there will be those who abuse these rights and sometimes blatantly so. But shutting them up is far more costly than tuning them out. It is the price we pay for freedom. Encouraging freedom of thought is no less important than freedom of speech.

While the patent system could certainly use some fixing, I would prefer it favour the patent holder to a fault than make stealing good ideas easier.

Value judgements

There are many overly broad patents. If the PTO refused to allow patents unless they met very narrow criteria, pretty soon, the invention stream would flow to a trickle. Placing a value judgement on what is innovation and who are serious inventors is more dangerous than it appears. I can understand people's impatience with overly broad patents. They can be abusive and frustrating. But narrowing issuance criteria too much would not be a step in the right direction.

Many patents are easy targets; broad ones are easier still. Taking cheap shots at otherwise acceptable inventions only proves that we need better dispute alternatives. When it comes to young industries – like the internet, software and biotech – innovations, at first, can be sweeping. When Edison was inventing, the fear was that he would control electricity. People thought Bell would dominate the telephone industry and undermine its development.

History shows that while the barriers to entry presented by some patents can be daunting, frequently they facilitate prosperity. While difficult to enforce, a peanut butter and jelly spreading invention may be just what a five-year old needs in the morning, and what his sleepy parents are willing to pay for.

From the ridiculous to the sublime

2007

Some patents are broad and difficult to enforce. It does not necessarily make them less valid or unimportant.

Narrower patents do not necessarily produce better inventions or more valuable rights. In my last column (IAM issue 20, page 21, "Dumb and dumber"), I considered patents on what appear to be ridiculous inventions, such as a "method of combing one's hair to conceal baldness". What do people whose business it is to obtain and monetise innovation think about narrowing the definition of what is considered inventive?

"I certainly do not want a government employee deciding what is important enough for patent protection," says Steven Rubin, a patent attorney at Wolf Block in New York told me recently. "As long as an invention meets the requirements for patentability, that it is new to the world, it should be awarded patent protection. The US courts and most others have generally agreed with this," he states.

"I remember an invention relating to the combination of peanut butter and jelly in one container," continues Rubin. "As a parent of a five-year old child who eats only five foods, one of which is PB&J sandwiches, such a combination is not a bad idea.

If the product is new to the market and it's profitable enough to incur a lawsuit, perhaps it is the type of thing worthy of patent protection. Just because it's simple doesn't mean it doesn't help science or society."

Patent worthy

"It is not up to us to decide what is worthy of a patent," argues Irving Rappaport, former chief patent counsel for Apple Computer, Medtronic and National Semiconductor, and co-founder with Kevin Rivette (chief IP strategist at IBM) of SmartPatents. "About 98% of patents turn out not to have any direct economic value, but that is not a reason to shut down the patent system. Since the USPTO is 100% funded by users and not taxpayers, why should anyone care? There are 400,000 applications a year being filed in the US and only about 2,500 patent infringement cases [of which fewer than 4% go to trial].

What is everyone so upset about?" Readers of this column (and my books) recall that I am fond of reminding them that the USPTO is a lot like another US government agency, the IRS. Almost any competent lawyer can get a patent to issue, just as most accountants who wish to can engineer a refund on an individual tax return. But a refund cheque does not mean that the tax filing will endure the scrutiny of an audit, which takes place on about 1.5% of returns. The percentage of patent suits that go to trial is between 3% and 4%. Still, to most taxpayers, the prospect of fines, back taxes and interest is sufficiently daunting to dissuade any bending of the rules. The government and society rely on them to act honourably. Similarly, government relies on patent applicants for a degree of sincerity and the courts to keep both infringers and filers honest.

Innovation can no more be legislated than good taste. Abusive patent filers can be as deceptive as tax cheats. Their actions foster a kind of cynicism that undermines both innovation and commerce. Jim Fergason is no cynic. He is among those independent inventors who know first-hand that the patent system can work. Fergason is responsible for discovering and commercialising the LCD (liquid crystal diode) used in hundreds of millions of watches and displays worldwide. His patents are used by nearly all LCD makers. He has been inducted into the USPTO Inventors Hall of Fame and was 2006 recipient of the US$500,000 Lemelson Prize from MIT, which he donated to charity. He grew up on a farm in Missouri and attended school in a one-room house. Fergason became wealthy not from inventing but from enforcing his rights, which he had to learn how to do when he saw companies infringing them.

"It doesn't hurt to issue what may appear to be a dumb patent," says Fergason. "It may hurt more not to issue it. Westinghouse developed a urinal many years ago that checked pH each time it flushed. Most people thought it was a big joke, but it can be used for dozens of tests. In hindsight many successful inventions appear to be ridiculously simple. Good patents can sometimes be broad."

Half of a hole

Patent prosecutor and strategist Brenda Pomerance thinks outrageous patents, including those on business methods, should be taken seriously.
"They remind me of a patent that I made fun of once. It was for a video cassette cartridge with a hole in it. 'Hole?' I scoffed, 'how could this rise to the level of an invention?' Well, it turned out that because of the hole, the loading/unloading mechanism could be built differently, enabling a low-profile VCR, which was indeed of commercial significance. So, you never know," she says.

"It's not the patent office's job to weed out silly stuff. Let it issue. In rare cases when it is necessary, the courts and the marketplace will figure it out," Pomerance continues. "Surely, among the over 7 million issued patents, a few blatantly silly ones are bound to get issued and even asserted. Many patents look like they read on serious inventions, but when you understand the technology that underlies them they can be just as silly in context. Dumb patents are like dumb people. There are always going to be some of them around."

When it comes to inventions and the claims on them, dumb is often is in the eye of the beholder. Many patents that appear to be about serious technology are often considered absurd by serious technologists in the field because they know they are obvious. But that does not mean they will never issue or not require vetting. Because everyone apparently is an expert on making sandwiches, the PB & J sandwich maker or business method patent appears stupid and obvious. The patent system's job is to encourage innovation. We should not be surprised, or angered, if it inadvertently promotes some nonsense along the way.

Friendly persuasion

2007

It is no secret that amicus filers are not always interested in the general cause of justice.

Amicus curiae (n) is Latin for "friend of the court". An amicus is filed when a party or an organisation wants to influence or otherwise participate in the argument regarding a case in which it is not one of the litigants. For those filing briefs, their own agenda is most important. A brief not only reveals a filer's perspective on matters of law but can provide investors with an indication of its relative IP strengths and weaknesses.

Two of the most significant IP cases in recent memory, eBay v MercExchange and KSR v Teleflex, both heard by the United States Supreme Court, attracted a rash of friends' briefs. The position of the filers was not as predictable as some had imagined – ample evidence of how rapidly the IP world is turning and what it is turning into.

eBay v MercExchange focused on the appropriateness of injunctive relief, especially if the plaintiff does not produce or practise a product associated with the infringed invention. Some say the Court's decision in this case effectively results in compulsory licensing, weakening patent holders' negotiating position and encouraging more litigation.

Dennis Crouch's Patently-O blog has linked the filings for your reading pleasure. I encourage you to peruse them. You will learn much about

On the merits	Hoffberg	"general rule" of granting injunctions)
Supporting MercExchange	**Supporting eBay (weaker injunctions)**	Fifty-two law professors (weaker
(strong injunctions)	Yahoo!	injunction provision)
US government	Electronic Frontier Foundation	Teva (weaker injunctions)
Intellectual Ventures and Inventors	Brief of Professors Pollack & Reynolds	Bar Assn of the District of Columbia
L&E Professors	Computer & Communications Industry	(cautioning about meddling in a
BIO	Association (CCIA)	political issue)
PhRMA	Brief of Intel, Microsoft, Oracle and Micron	IBM (equitable principles must be examined)
Brief of GE, 3M, P&G Du Pont and J&J	Securities Industry Association	
Qualcomm	Research-In-Motion	**Briefs for/against certiorari**
Rembrandt IP Management	Nokia	Professors' brief (includes Lemley,
University of California and other	Bar of the City of New York	Samuelson & Lessig)
research universities	Business Software Alliance (BSA) Brief	eBay brief
AAU	Time Warner, et al	MercExchange brief
United Inventors		CCIA (Computers & Communications
ABA	**Supporting neither party**	Industry Association)
Franklin Pierce law professors	AIPLA & FCBA joint brief (supporting a	EFF (Electronic Frontier Foundation)
		Qualcomm

how some companies regard their IP assets and how they might use them (http://patentlaw.typepad.com/patent/2006/03/ebay_v_mercexch.html)

James D Woods, a PhD economist for Grant Thornton in Houston and an IP valuation expert, says that a company's amicus brief often is informed by how an industry captures innovation. "Pharma companies typically want fewer, stronger patents and the ability to file injunctions against generic makers who they feel may be infringing," he says. "High-tech producers, on the other hand, rely on larger numbers of questionably valid patents that may have an ambiguous relationship with the products they may relate to. Large-tech companies can be severely damaged by small patent owners and independent inventors, as well as trolls. There are numerous possibilities for infringing patents relating to a camcorder or financial service product, many fewer for a gas turbine or blockbuster drug."

The upshot of the attempts to influence the courts through friendly opinions is that some patentees, such as smaller companies, independent inventors and investors, would like to retain strong patent protection. Larger portfolio owners tend to adhere to the notion that patents are best granted but not used. Why then did such IP giants as GE, 3M and P&G weigh in for Teleflex, while Cisco and GM were on the side of narrow interpretation, ironically, along with the patent-suspicious Electronic Frontier Foundation and Intel? What about Intellectual Ventures' investors, among them Sony, Google, Nokia and Microsoft? Are they attempting to play on both sides simultaneously?

The IP world is changing rapidly. Companies of all sizes and types have a need to realise greater returns on innovation. Monetisation strategies are complex and what served one company's (or industry's) interest 10 years ago may not do so today and will not tomorrow. It appears the US courts want to make it harder for some to monetise patents. Amicus filers weighing in on the debate are providing financial analysis as well as judicial perspective. Smart investors will read between the lines.

Talking monkeys

2007

What is it that makes otherwise intelligent people appear to be Neanderthals when it comes to IP?

One of the most successful entertainers of our time, Michael Crichton, is the author of *Jurassic Park* and 14 other best-selling novels. His latest, *Next*, deals with the destruction wrought by gene patents. Thirteen of his novels have been made into films, several of which he directed, and he is creator of one of the most successful series on television, *ER*. He is the only creative to have running simultaneously a number one film, novel and television series.

However, there is another, darker side to this Hollywood success story. Dr Crichton, a Harvard-trained MD who did post-doctoral work at the Salk Institute and has taught anthropology at Cambridge University, has been mixing IP fact with fiction.

In The New York Times, which I urge you all to all read (http://www.nytimes.com/2007/02/13/opinion/13crichton.html?ex=11 72552400&en=c09a391fb5085528&ei=5070), he vents his spleen about the societal dangers of providing exclusivity for gene-related inventions. What he writes is clearly the product of a creative mind run amok; or perhaps, he is seeking to encourage controversy in support of a personal agenda, such as book sales.

Pirates of the human genome

"Gene patents are now used to halt research, prevent medical testing and keep vital information from you and your doctor," Dr Crichton writes. "Gene patents slow the pace of medical advances on deadly diseases. And they raise costs exorbitantly; a test for breast cancer that could be done for $1,000 now costs $3,000."

He tells the reader that this is "because the holder of the gene patent can charge whatever he wants, and does. Couldn't somebody make a cheaper test? Sure, but the patent holder blocks any competitor's test. He owns the gene. Nobody else can test for it."

Apparently, this is all the fault of the USPTO: "This bizarre situation has come to pass because of a mistake by an underfinanced and understaffed government agency. The United States Patent Office misinterpreted previous Supreme Court rulings and some years ago began — to the surprise of everyone, including scientists decoding the genome — to issue patents on genes."

But, according to Crichton it gets even worse: "In addition, a gene's owner can in some instances also own the mutations of that gene, and these mutations can be markers for disease... Today, more than 20 human pathogens are privately owned, including haemophilus influenza and Hepatitis C."

I blinked after reading the above statements and emailed a few people for a reality check. Gene-related inventions are and should be patentable; if the patents covering some of them were granted in error, the courts will invalidate them. If they are not, they are sure to inspire a lot of important research in adjacent areas.

This was the response about the editorial that I received from Bruce Lehman, former United States Commissioner of Patents and Trademarks:

"I have read several of his novels, and while entertaining, they are hardly serious literature. I don't think he knows anything about patent law.

You are correct that the patent does not cover the actual genes in the body – there must be a utility to the patent. Certainly, using knowledge of a gene to develop a test for a disease is something that involves the kind of R&D that should be supported by the patent system. The testing procedure could be novel and non-obvious and, therefore, appropriately patentable. There seems to be a disturbing trend lately to think that it is immoral somehow to get paid for inventions that result from R&D in the health sciences. To the extent that patients cannot afford new treatments, that is not a patent issue – but a safety net issue that needs to be addressed with remedies such as the new (US) Medicare Part D system."

Out of control

Irving Rappaport, former chief patent counsel at Apple, National Semiconductor and Medtronic, provides similar perspective: "I read Crichton's most recent book, Next, which deals with patents. I thought it was one of his poorer books. The story line has talking monkeys and birds around which he weaves a fantastic, but unbelievable, tale about how gene research gets out of control and affects unrelated families across the country. He did go to medical school, about 40 years ago, and then became a writer. Someone must have put a bee under his bonnet about gene-related patents and he has gotten on a high horse to speak to the masses based on little experience in the patent field. His article shows the dangers of a layman talking about a field of which he knows nothing. He should stick to writing novels and TV shows, for which he has some ability. Maybe his latest book sales are down and he is looking for some free publicity to pump them up."

In response to Dr Crichton's op-ed, John F Duffy, a research professor at George Washington University Law School, said in a letter to the editor that "gene patents have the same effect as all patents: they temporarily increase prices to provide greater incentives for discovery. It would be no less true and no less hyperbolic to speculate that you, or someone you love, could die if genes became unpatentable because the necessary genetic research would not be done in time."

Copy and sell

A final sobering thought came from op-ed responder David P Lentini, a patent attorney in San Francisco: "Gene patents are vital to the biotechnology and pharmaceutical industries. Why would anyone risk the billions needed to transform basic science into lifesaving products if someone else could simply copy those products without risk? I doubt that Michael Crichton would let others copy and sell his novels and movies for no cost."

From my perspective, the greater threat to our well-being is less likely to come from gene patents than from entertainers, politicians, healthcare professionals, and the like, with a little knowledge and too much imagination. Dinosaurs 1, humans 0.

IP bonds 2.0

2007

The largest ever IP-backed securitisation, US$1.8 billion for Sears' Kenmore, Craftsman and DieHard brands, may be a harbinger of things to come for IP as an asset class and for financial markets flush with capital.

A new generation of IP bonds has been born. These bear only a passing resemblance to the royalty-backed Bowie bonds which were issued in 1997. That instrument relied on a stream of projected income from copyrighted songs to make the lender whole. My understanding is that Sears' brand-name bonds do not involve any pre-existing royalty payments.

Contrary to popular belief, monetising IP is not alchemy. Properly structured, IP financings can unlock value that markets and capital providers have overlooked. But while interest in IP assets is healthy, too much capital chasing the wrong rights is not. It's up to the financial markets to divine the logic of this transaction, but my money is on Sears' reputation for dependability.

The story broke in *Business Week* in the middle of April and much of the press picked up on how Sears "quietly created" the mechanism for transforming its Kenmore, Craftsman and Die Hard brands into a financial security. Eric Hedman, an analyst at S&P, which like *Business Week* is owned by McGraw-Hill, called it the largest IP loan ever.

Wide impact

The structure and intent of these bonds are worth examining. This transaction affects every large IP owner and investor, especially stakeholders in innovative companies.

It has been widely reported that Sears Holdings Corp (NYSE:SHLD) CEO Edward Lambert wants to recast its floundering retailing giants Sears and Kmart in the image of Warren Buffet's value-laden Berkshire Hathaway. But what has actually happened?

The bonds, as I understand them, did not leave control of the company. They are being held in Sears' Bermuda-based insurance subsidiary. According to *Business Week*, Sears first created KCD, a "separate, wholly owned, bankruptcy-remote subsidiary" (sometimes known as a special purpose entity or IP holding company). This is not at all unique and many significant IP holders establish SPEs primarily for tax purposes, but also to control operating company cash flows and profit. KCD issued the bonds that are being held by the Bermuda insurer. Sears is licensing the brands from its own sub, presumably to provide the Bermuda entity with assets but not income because Sears pays no royalties.

With a stronger balance sheet than Sears Holdings', the Bermuda insurer which it controls, or KCD, is in position to engage in financial engineering that could benefit the operating company. (The bonds are worth more on the sub's balance sheet than on Sears'.) In fact, the KCD bonds are rated by Moody's Investor Service four rungs better than Sears' junk debt. Through KCD, Sears can issue debt and use the funds to acquire an insurer or for other leverage. For Sears equity holders, this creates opportunity; for its secured debt holders, the re-capitalisation is less positive. They can no longer rely upon the company's crown jewel assets in the event of a bankruptcy. But then again, in that scenario those assets are not likely to be valued at US$1.8 billion.

Why do it, then? Todd Sullivan, editor of Seeking Alpha, an investment blog (http://retail.seekingalpha.com/article/31960\) responds thoughtfully to that question:

1. *Sell the bonds to outsiders.* Then, Sears would be holding up to $1.8 billion in cash, and investors would be holding the bonds.
2. *License the brands.* Many people [Sullivan included] feel there is a huge revenue stream for Sears in the value of these brands. Allowing outside manufacturers to make products and use the Craftsman, Kenmore and Diehard brand names in return for royalty payments is an easy way to increase profits without any additional expense. These payments would be virtually 100% profit for Sears.
3. *Swap bonds for debt.* Lampert acquired K Mart through its debt. These new "brand" bonds allow him a vehicle to do a similar deal. How? Lampert could swap these bonds or a portion of them for the debt of another company. One morning a shareholder of BJ's could wake up and find that Sears Holdings owns all his or her debt... Having these bonds as leverage also allows for the possibility of a much larger acquisition.
4. *Insurance.* Now we have an insurance subsidiary of Sears sitting there holding $1.8 billion in bonds that could be used for an acquisition... few acquisitions would make the stock price of SHLD explode to the upside   more   than   the   purchasing   of   an   insurer.

New era

However Sears chooses to deploy the assets resulting from capitalising its leading brands, one thing is certain: under-leveraged IP rights have entered a new era.

The investment community has come a long way since the appearance of music royalty bonds. While much attention was heaped on these early IP instruments, some of their cash flow projections proved overly zealous in the face of technological advances, such as the iPod. Not faring much better was the securitisation of patent royalties from Bristol-Myer's Squibb's HIV drug Zerit, invented by Yale university researchers. The Sears bonds represent a major step forward for IP not only because of their size, but because of their structure and apparent flexibility. They not only capitalise otherwise underutilised intangible assets, poorly reflected on the company's balance sheet, but could provide the beleaguered company with additional resources that can make it more competitive.

I believe the Sears transaction also is significant for certain strategic invention rights, namely patents. While patents without royalty streams are harder to value than marks, lenders are starting to become comfortable with them. If the rights to unlicensed brands are creditworthy, patents or families of patents that make companies more competitive will eventually be recognised, too. Time will tell.

Performance anxiety

2007

When it comes to understanding what innovation rights such as patents mean to public company performance, CEOs are hiding in plain sight.

A business's huge investment in innovation deeply affects its bottom line. Still, patents for most global 1000 managements are apparently too elusive to get a handle on. In fairness, there are few reliable measures of patent performance. Accounting for their complex strengths is demanding. But if executives give up trying, failure may open the door for regulators and others. The US Supreme Court is already looking into patent quality and strategy. The lack of benchmarks may also lead to shareholder suits or activist investors who wish to replace managements or join them on the board.

Ignorance about how rights perform is no excuse. This is a potentially risky and sometimes coy response to patents' complexity and purpose that discourages honest discussion about how businesses are best run. IP managers have not been much help. However, unlike CEOs, CFOs and boards of directors, they are not responsible for generating shareholder value. Companies must realise that the failure to understand patent performance sends the wrong message to investors and others.

It implies that measuring the impact of innovation is outside of their realm, impossible or unnecessary. Some believe that litigation is the only real way to identify most important inventions and that other methods are too subjective or insufficiently rigorous.

Revenue quality

Many companies report informally about their patent royalties because it is a relatively simple matter. They represent payments in exchange for the right to use an invention. Patent royalties are much higher-quality revenue than product sales and licensors are fond of reminding us of this. Marshall Phelps, now chief of IP strategy at Microsoft, told me that when he ran IBM's licensing programme in the 1990s, margins on royalties were better than 95%. That's performance by any standard. This may be music to a CEO's ears. But what about companies that successfully deploy patents without generating royalties?

How do we know what their IP is contributing to the bottom line? While for some, invention success may equate to royalty streams, for others it may reflect improved market share, profit margins or freedom to operate – and how do you value those attributes? Very carefully, is my guess.

One measure

Patent licensing is only one measure of R&D performance, management skill and financial results. At ratings agencies Standard & Poor's and Moody's, cash flow or royalty streams are what really matter when it comes to modelling IP assets for securitisation. Other measures that should be applied to patent performance are not always readily apparent or relevant to credit analysis. These include patents' role in achieving or maintaining: market share (freedom of action); profit margins; product sales; customer relationships (sales); M&A; shareholder value; reputation; and capital formation.

We recently posted on the Brody Berman Associates website a graph. I call it "IP Profit in Perspective".

Patent licensing revenue as a percentage
of net profit 2006

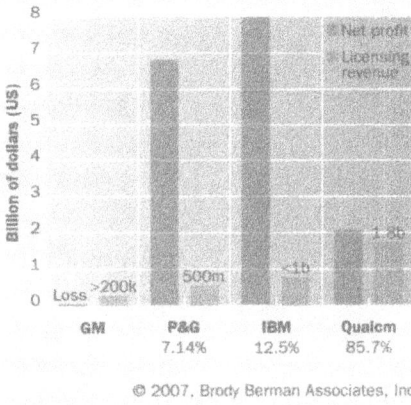

© 2007, Brody Berman Associates, Inc

It represents patent licensing revenue as a percentage of four large companies' net profit. The graph illustrates the importance of patent royalties to overall company profitability. The companies were selected because they represent fairly diverse patentees and industries.

Troubled General Motors has some licensing income (estimated) which contributes a small amount to its beleaguered bottom line. P&G, long associated with consumer bands (Tide®, etc), has come to rely on patent licensing to produce company-wide financial results. More than 7% of its net profit comes from patent licensing. IBM, long seen as a poster child for IP, provides 12.5% of its net-net via IP licensing (some of this is copyright and brand-related licensing). The irony is that household products giant P&G is now relying on patent licensing in much the same way that high-tech leader IBM does. When it comes to Qualcomm, which manufactures few, if any, products, company performance is mostly about patent licensing. Royalties comprise 85.7% of its net profit and about one-third of its overall income

Getting atop the bottom line

There is an extraordinary need to quantify the role of invention rights in profitability and the creation of shareholder value. The particular method I have suggested is only one. (In future IP Investor columns I hope to discuss others). Most agree that patent count is among the weakest measures. Patent citations may show relevance to an area of technology or PTO classification, but they do not convey patents' complex role in company success or stock price. For now, even a weak measure would be better than none. CEOs: come out, come out wherever you are.

Flatter and faster

2008

For companies pursuing open innovation, providing access to IP rights is about business, not good citizenship.

Investors are trying to sort out how open innovation (OI) makes sense to intellectual property owners. The geography of innovation has shifted, but companies remain uncertain about how best to map it.

In a flatter environment, ideas are exchanged readily over wide spaces. Profit and speed, not control, are emerging as key enablers. But while OI sounds more politically correct, and while it may facilitate a leveller playing field, it also means more opportunities for a wider range of patent holders.

Despite this, *The Economist*, which usually does a good job of identifying technology trends, recently wrote that patents have become less important. In an otherwise thoughtful special report on innovation that all but ignored IP rights, the magazine said that shifts in information and ideas, such as those that Tom Friedman popularised in The World is Flat, have made IP less meaningful to developing and developed nations.

Transforming entire industries

In one of the supplement's six articles, "The love-in", correspondent

Vijay Vaitheeswaran contends that the move towards open innovation is beginning to transform entire industries and it is minimising the role of patents.

"For one thing," he writes, "patents are becoming much less important than brands and the speed at which products can be got to market. It is true that some of the rising stars in developing economies are beginning to take out more patents, but many of their innovations are still kept quiet as trade secrets. So fluid are their markets, and so weak the historical patent protection in them, that bosses often prefer to keep things in the dark – and come up with the next innovation as necessary to stay ahead of the competition."

Vaitheeswaran fails to point out that more brands today are based on or complemented by proprietary technology, namely patents and trade secrets. Individual inventors and small businesses in developing nations can compete successfully for patent rights in developed ones, where the pay-off can be more significant than it is currently at home. Japan had little interest in patents in the 1960s; Korea in the 1980s. Today, they are among the world's most active filers, especially in the US.

"Even in developed markets, the acceleration of innovation is making patents less relevant," Vaitheeswaran continues. "What is more, say brand experts at P&G (which claims not even to count patents any longer), the dizzying pace of change today confuses consumers with a baffling array of choices. Such firms are increasingly turning to trusted brands to simplify things."

Selective collaboration

Yes, accessibility to innovation and collaboration are more appealing than exclusivity or monopoly – words often associated with patents. But players still must be discriminating. Open innovation means selective collaboration. Doing more and broader in-licensing, joint ventures, patent purchases and standards setting works only if it makes business sense for parties to do so.

An early proponent of open innovation was Gillette. In the early 1900s it decided to establish a standard by giving away perfectly sellable razor blades to move more shavers. Today, Gillette (now owned by P&G) still is open sourcing the razors and selling the shavers. In the same way, companies such as IBM and Microsoft give customers, vendors and even competitors more access to certain innovation assets. The reasons include setting standards to speed products to market, providing the basis for know-how licensing or lucrative consulting contracts, saving R&D costs, and (yes) engaging in patent licensing activity.

Good ideas today are more likely to come from diverse sources, especially India and China. Companies are just starting to learn how to tap these veins of innovation.

In one of *The Economist* articles, Unilever executive David Dunce says: "Twelve years ago, when I joined [the company], we were very closed, vertically integrated and owned more of the value chain – even the chemicals and software we used … Now, [Unilever] is much more receptive to ideas and services from outside, even posting challenges on the Internet for people to come up with new ideas." More than 40% of the new products P&G launched in 2006 have key elements that originated from outside of the company. By comparison, the amount was 15% in 2000.

Bringing down costs

Open innovation is not charity, nor should it be. Large companies need to encourage broader collaboration because it brings down costs and creates more opportunities. But they still need to manage their patent estate closely.

If anything, patents are more important today, because of increases in in- and out-licensing, joint ventures and collaboration.

The pharmaceutical industry may be somewhat ahead of the curve on collaboration. It learned decades ago that spending, say, US$3 billion in annual R&D expenditures to ensure a pipeline of blockbuster drugs is a lot, but nowhere near enough. Even US$30 billion would not do it. Hence, drug companies tend to use their research dollars efficiently, identifying areas of interest, inventions they may need to in-license, and which patents or companies it makes sense to buy. They know they cannot survive without partners.

The day of the self-contained R&D engine – such as Watson Research Center and Bell Labs – may be drawing to a close. The geography of innovation, fuelled by more and cheaper researchers and high-speed communications, is reshaping the avenues for new ideas. By drawing upon the best work from a variety of sources, OI creates a more robust market for business and for IP rights alike.

OI also means that inventors and companies had better learn how to protect their ideas before deciding where, how, and with whom they want to share them. It is no mystery why companies that are bastions of proprietary innovation are now also promoting collaboration.

Restless natives

2008

There are more ways to make money from IP rights than ever before. The key is identifying which ones are right for you.

The business executives, patent owners and investors I speak to share similar concerns regarding IP rights. They want to know the best ways to generate return on patents, as well as how to avoid litigation – something that has become increasingly complex. Most companies today are content to deploy their patents for freedom to operate – to sell their products without encumbrances, such as threat of an injunction or costly law suit. And they are satisfied with the ROI on IP (or ROIP) generated by using their patents defensively.

But not all patent owners agree this is the only, or best, approach. There are essentially two kinds of IP investor: strategic and direct. Strategic investors are generally companies with large portfolios that are more interested in freedom to operate and leveraging the power of their IP, than in generating cash flows from licensing royalties. Direct investors, however, regard IP as financial assets to be sliced, diced, arbitraged and, when necessary, asserted legally for maximum return. They are unconcerned about counter-assertion because they sell no products. Their sole product is licensing, which frequently is accompanied by litigation. Below is a summary of alternative methods of extracting value from IP which, for the most part, do not involve litigation.

IP loans

Small to mid-sized businesses with modest but established product or company brand names can sometimes borrow on those assets without diluting equity. They don't have to be Coke or McDonald's to do this. However, they do need a recognisable presence within their industry. To be collateralised, a brand need not necessarily be licensed for use by others (e.g. Wise potato chips, BCBG Max Azria fashion line). However, those that are licensed and generating cash flow are generally more appealing to lenders.

Royalty stream sales

Patents that generate reliable cash flow from licensing can be used to create a securitised asset. For licensors willing to take a discount on the projected cash flow over a period of time, say five years, the upfront lump-sum payment can pay a lot of bills. It also can mitigate the risk inherent in high-tech licensing. In a securitisation, the creditworthiness of the licensee is much more a factor than that of the patent, trademark or copyright owner. IP royalty streams have been securitised for music royalties, university inventions and other cash-generating IP assets. They are similar to a real estate sale-leaseback, which permits the use of the asset by the seller. Highly creditworthy companies with a low cost of capital are generally less interested in securitisation.

Patent sales

Over the past two or three years a significant market for the sale of invention rights or patents has emerged. While values are not always what sellers expect, they are creeping upwards. Even unlicensed, un-infringed patents that are not being used (especially those relating to the high-tech fields) can fetch anywhere from US$10,000 to US$50,000. Stronger patents that are being infringed, or may be in the future, can fetch as much as US$1 million or more. Sellers must be realistic about what they are offering and should expect to give huge discounts on patents with 'potential' value due to the cost and risk involved for the buyer; monetising the asset then becomes his or her gamble. Typical patent buyers include brokers representing large companies looking to beef up their portfolios and speculators, sometimes known as trolls.

Equity sale to IP-centric investors

This is the newest twist on one of the oldest forms of IP investing. Private equity or other investors take a position in a public (or private) operating company whose fate is tied significantly to its innovation. The play here is that if the company does well, the investor makes a handsome return on the stock. If it does not, the patent or other IP rights may be able to be asserted, licensed, sold or otherwise monetised. It's all about the quality of the patent rights and the ability to extract value from them. Public companies that are IP-centric in nature include InterDigital, Tessera, Qualcomm, Rambus and Mosaid. Private ones are too numerous to mention.

Licensing/litigation partners

In high-tech, and to a much lesser extent in bio-pharma, few infringers will take an expensive licence unless forced to. This can mean high legal fees and long timeframes, especially when the defendant is large and well capitalised. Many direct investors and law firms (who also are IP investors) prey on such disputes. Few banks and traditional lenders will fund patent litigation. As a result, participation equity is attractive and returns high for those with patience and strong stomachs. Players include law firms such as McCool Smith and Niro Scavone, as well as brand-name players such as Baker & Botts and Kirkland Ellis. Patient private equity investors with the appropriate time horizon are also playing. While some refer to these speculators as trolls, there is no denying that regarding patent rights for their potential cash value, despite recent US court decisions, is still lucrative to some.

More opportunities

Banks and financial institutions still have a hard time determining what patents and other IP rights are worth today, let alone what they will be in the future. Speciality lenders, buyers and investors have emerged who see opportunity where others see confusion. By balancing risk with reward, they will pay cash for even partial ownership in the right patent or patents. Ten years from now, sellers in a more efficient market will undoubtedly get better prices for their IP assets. However, things are looking up. Today's market is much more viable than just two years ago. More opportunities exist today for inventors, investors and businesses of all sizes to generate better returns on a broader range of innovation rights. Long may it continue.

Investormania

2008

Businesses are attempting to figure out just who or what is an IP investor and whether they all are equally deserving of ROI, as we know it.

Intellectual property rights are finally being recognised as business assets. We have all heard that the estimated market value of intangibles in companies that comprise the S&P 500 exceeds 75% and that IP rights play a highly significant role in the success of almost every business, including those less obviously dependent on innovation and technology. Given companies' commitment to R&D, capturing value associated with innovation is a high priority (sample 2007 R&D spending for innovative companies: US$8.03 billion for Microsoft; US$10.61 billion for Pfizer; and US$7.17 billion for Daimler-Chrysler AG).

Explosive technology growth in the 1980s, coupled with record patent infringement awards and high defence costs, have fuelled interest in IP rights. But investing in IP conjures a shadowy image of outsiders speculating on grants of exclusivity some feel they have no right to. It also challenges us to look at what is expedient for shareholders and society, and what are ethical business practices. Today, there are many kinds of IP investors with a wide range of expectations. They all require some form of ROI, but they differ radically on how they achieve it and the footprint that they leave behind.

Catalysts for change?

Non-practising owners who speculate on IP rights and assert them against risk adverse operating companies – however they may be regarded – have been a catalyst for change. But what are the most efficient ways for companies to invent, secure rights and turn the rights into productive assets? IP investors come in many shapes and sizes, and even those that create pain can serve a purpose. The right IP rights, especially the right patents, increasingly have been seen as valuable resources, even if they cannot be readily captured and valued like real estate and other tangibles.

Not everyone agrees that using patents for direct return and measuring their performance in terms of licensing revenue generated facilitates innovation or long-term business objectives. The framers of the US Constitution had unusually high respect for the rights or innovators, such as inventors and authors. While they could not foresee the complex financial engineering that would take place starting in the 20th century, they did anticipate the impact that rights could have on a broad range of businesses and how that could affect America's competitiveness.

The jury is still out on whether the returns on direct IP investing justify the investment. How should we measure return on an IP investment (ROIP)? R&D, legal costs and filing fees do not come cheap. Which IP owners are better off licensing their best patents to others, even competitors, while they still can, rather than using them for freedom to sell products? These are difficult calls, and, unfortunately, ones that senior management loath to make. Company executives tend to play a passive role in IP decision making, sometimes to the detriment of shareholders. IP is abstract, context-dependent and ever-changing. CEOs are trained in business schools to manage resources such as products and people, and tangibles such as real estate, that can be identified on balance sheets and scrutinised by shareholders. They are at a loss when it comes to dealing with intangibles like IP. But with the advent of senior IP executives such as Marshall Phelps at Microsoft and Joe Beyers at HP, effectively CIPOs or Chief IP Officers, the picture is improving.

Direct IP Investors (Source: Corporate Deal Maker and Brody Berman Associates)

Investor	Founded	Capital (USD millions)
Intellectual Ventures	2000	1000+
Acacia Technologies	2001	400
Rembrandt Group	2003	150
Ocean Tomo Capital Fund	2005	200
Altitude Capital Partners	2005	250
Deutsche Bank Patent Fund	2006	210
Paradox Capital	2006	280
Coller Capital	2006	200
IP-Com (Fortress)	2006	???

Few rights are assets

C-level execs and Wall Street consistently fail to realise that only a handful of patent rights are financial assets. For a patent to be an asset, strategic or otherwise, a galaxy of stars and planets must align. In a high-tech company with some 10,000 patents, fewer than 5%, by most estimates, and as little as 2%, have discernible value. Perhaps 45% of the rights are necessary for future uses and for bargaining leverage (cross-licensing or counter-assertion, should it be necessary) and future uses, while the remaining 50% or so have no value and are typically allowed to lapse. Two out of every three patents lapse because of failure to pay fees. It is not that the owners lack the funds to pay the renewals, or forget to. At a point it makes little sense to do so.

Pharmaceutical company patent portfolios are much smaller than those in the high-tech industries. Typically, a formulation will be covered by a single patent or a few patents, eliminating the need for a lot of patent filing or cross-licences. Also, validity is less of an issue for most bio-pharma patents. Finally, it is relatively easy for small companies or individuals to invent, file, secure and even buy high-tech patents. It is a different matter in the pharma industry, where access to tools and significant capital is required. Whatever the industry or context, IP investing is a full-contact sport that requires deep pockets, calm nerves and patience.

Jungle logic

2008

If value in the property market is all about location, in the patent market it is all about context.

New York, spring 2008 ... The sub-prime mortgage crisis arrived in New York with a bang. Just across from my office is the new Bear Stearns building, where investment bankers mill about the entrance and smoke cigarettes, silently calculating their remaining net worth. The sub-prime meltdown has reaffirmed the three cardinal rules of real estate transactions: "Location, location, location." It also serves to remind us of the top priorities for patent assets: "Context, context, context."

A patent is 100% of something. Rarely is this as grandiose as it sounds. Mostly, that something the patent encompasses is worth, er, well... nothing. It's like owning a 500 square mile tract in Siberia. Yes, you may hold the title to a large expanse of land, but unless a lot of oil is found there and it can be accessed, it is not worth the paper the title is written on; 500 square feet in central London, Manhattan or Tokyo, however, is another matter. A patent is not unlike a mining claim. It is all about knowing where and when to place the stakes. Stake it too broadly and it will be too difficult to defend; too narrowly and it may not cover anything worthwhile; too early and it may go unnoticed. A few miles, and sometimes a few yards, can make all of the difference in the world.

For a patent to have licensing value, it not only needs to be well-configured and prosecuted, but one or more of its claims needs actually to read on an invention that generates significant revenue. Simply put, it needs to be valid and seriously infringed. For strategic patents, the standard of measurement is more abstract. Their significant value may be internal and untested in the courts or in the marketplace. A well-rendered patent whose claims read on a product with weak sales is not very meaningful; neither is a poorly researched and configured one that reads on a successful product. What has meaning is a patent (better still, a family of patents) whose claims read directly on an invention which has been successfully commercialised and whose products have been selling well in the marketplace. However, establishing a strong fact pattern of infringement is no guarantee of reward because of the substantial cost, time and risk required to prove it.

Uneasy money

At a median cost of US$4.5 million (for cases with US$25 million or more at stake), and as high as US$62 million for an unusual and protracted case – such as the US$1.4 billion trial won in 2005 by Kirkland & Ellis for Karlin Medical Technologies – patent suits remain a viable way to deploy some infringed patent owners' time and money. The operative word is some. To prevail regularly in patent litigation you need to be selective, deep-pocketed, lucky and patient – no matter how strong the patent or how obvious the infringement.

Building a large and expansive patent portfolio is no assurance that any of its rights will read on the products they sell. In fact, frequently they do not. This leaves many operating companies vulnerable to patent suits and damages awards. Some NPEs (non-practising entities) and others attempt to exploit these weaknesses. Vulnerability to NPEs is compounded by USPTO, EPO and JPO pendency, where it can take five years or longer for some patents to issue; and when they do they are of dubious reliability. Patent examination costs and a lack of skilled examiners are among the forces at work here.

Smart choices

By the time an invention goes to market, the importance of a patent originally designated to protect it may have diminished significantly or even disappeared. As inventions evolve into commercialised products the patents originally filed to cover them may become irrelevant. The claims contained in a patent filed on the initial invention may differ from those necessary to protect the product actually sold. This can leave conscientious companies vulnerable and frustrated. Businesses need to keep their perspective regarding not only what IP coverages they have secured through R&D and internal patent filings, but also which ones they may need and do not have.

"Context, context, context"

Weak Patent A Reads on
Strong Patent B Reads on

Intel Pentium®D Processor
2005 Sales = $2 billion

Strong Patent C Reads on

Brand "Y" Processor
2005 Sales = $100+

Location means practically everything in
real estate; with intangible assets like patents
it is all about context

Where some see innovation as a jungle, others see it as an eco-system requiring interaction for survival of the species. It is becoming increasingly difficult for innovative companies to get by through burying their head in the sand, especially when they have weapons at their disposal, such as patent acquisitions, licensing and standards setting. Just ask Research in Motion. After paying out more than US$600 million in a settlement some say it could have secured for US$50 million, the Canadian firm has recently purchased a total of almost US$300 million in GPS and other patents. When it comes to IP rights, smart choices are sometimes painful ones. Senior managements seem determined to learn that lesson the hard way.

Measures of success

2008

Innovation profoundly affects every business and investor. While most executives believe that new ideas are the currency of choice, few agree on the best ways to profit from them.

In *From Assets to Profits,* my new book to be published in October, contributors explore how invention rights become business assets and the ways they can be converted into return. They confront questions facing managers and businesses that rely on innovation. These questions include:

- When do IP rights such as patents become assets?
- What are the best business models for a particular IP holder to achieve return or advantage?
- Who, in fact, are IP investors and how do they affect innovation?

IP value typically escapes the balance sheet. Revenues from patent licences are attractive to some because they are easily understood. But royalty generation is one of many ways intellectual assets can be monetised. It is not the definitive way. Many companies under pressure to perform get sucked into the competition to build patent stockpiles and generate fees. Some have called licensing income an addiction, a mythological siren song that seduces otherwise intelligent CEOs.

Return on intellectual assets means different things to different IP holders. The dynamics of deploying invention rights have changed dramatically over the past 20 years and there is a burden on patent owners today to extract meaningful returns on the high cost of R&D. This is especially true of operating companies that are engaged in selling products as opposed to licensing them. It is difficult to pinpoint the role IP rights play in protecting products' market share or maintaining their profit margins. It is even more difficult to capture their impact on overall business performance. A company may know that some of its patents vaguely support objectives, but seldom can it measure their impact on profitability, the lifeblood of a company.

Useful consequences

Wikipedia defines profit as "the making of gain in business activity for the benefit of the owners of the business". The word comes from Latin, meaning "to make progress", and is defined in two different ways, one for economics and one for accounting. "A key difficulty in measuring either definition of profit," notes Wikipedia "is in defining costs". I would add that another challenge is identifying advantage. Another definition of profit from BrainyQuote is also worth considering: "Accession of good; valuable results; useful consequences; benefit; avail; gain; as, an ounce of profit."

Unfortunately, there is currently no line on a 10-K report called "useful consequences". Goodwill does even less to explain things. IP value is a relative term that depends on context for meaning. Defining it in terms of royalties generated or damages awards won is too narrow for most IP holders. The patent revenue model is a very nasty business, often accompanied by disputes, distraction from day-to-day business and expensive litigation. The economics of licensing may work for some IP holders, but it is not right for the majority. For most companies, IP supports the business; for a few, it is the business.

Royalties are typically high-margin cash flows that both C-level executives and credit ratings agencies respond to. Strategic patent advantage is vague and abstract. The formidable challenge faced by CEOs and their advisers is how to capture and articulate the meaning of strategic advantage and translate it into the language of income statements and balance sheets. Without a fiscal handle on intellectual assets, otherwise ethical fiduciaries run the risk of mismanaging valuable assets, undermining return and facing regulatory scrutiny and shareholder suits. Settling a case for US$50 million, as RIM could have in 2002, is a better management decision than having to pay US$612 million three years later.

How businesses choose to use their patents is often determined by industry, size and willingness to do battle for what is theirs.

Uncertainty about patent validity and value, and the lack of pricing transparency, inhibit IP transactions. They in turn create market inefficiencies that are good for buyers, bad for sellers and hard on valuations. A surge in patent brokerage and auction activity is beginning to create a more efficient market for IP-related deals, including mergers and acquisitions.

Model behaviour

Some readers will view From Assets to Profits as a cautionary tale, an ode to strategic IP representing a move back to basics when patent rights were viewed as defensive shields. Others will see it as a call to manage innovation more imaginatively and globally. Still others will conclude that it is a rationale for speculators. The truth is that all are correct.

It is apparent that innovation exists less within a jungle of competing rights and more in a balanced ecosystem that relies on symbiosis as much as natural selection. Some of those operating in this environment, such as trolls, may appear to be less savoury characters than others. But like the "good" bacteria that inhabit one's digestive tract, some do serve a healthy purpose. Survival in the IP world is complex and requires competition to ensure quality and positive outcomes. Identifying, nurturing, acquiring, measuring, conveying and profiting from intellectual assets are in their infancy. As IP management matures, it is becoming clearer there are many ways to generate a return, but that some are more difficult to discern than others.

The CEO challenge

2008

As new patterns of IP exploitation emerge, the onus is on investors and corporate decision makers to make sure they do not miss the opportunities.

Inventing today is faster and more essential to economic survival than at any time in history. Proprietary research centres such as Lucent's Bell Labs and IBM's Watson, still bastions of ideas, may no longer be the best sources of business innovation. Some argue that the days of those once-revered invention factories may be numbered.

Outsourcing and better communications have changed how businesses generate new ideas. In what author and *New York Times* columnist Tom Friedman calls a "flatter" world, innovation can be organised and secured more readily from diverse sources at lower cost. Most large companies, even those that actively license, have a fundamentally different way of looking at rights from smaller entities or independent inventors. Operating companies have to be careful about who they enforce against because of possible counter-assertion and because they are loath to mistreat customers who may be infringing. But being mindful of assertion does not mean they can be complacent about where to secure the rights they need or think they might.

One of a business's greatest strengths today is the ability to recognise when intellectual rights – its own and others' – become intangible assets. There is a disconnect between relative patent value, which is its meaning to its owner, and market value – what a buyer is willing to pay for it. The market for transacting IP rights is still highly fragmented and inefficient, but it is improving. The threat of costly litigation – still a powerful inducement for settling disputes – and recent court decisions and proposed patent reform are making alternative strategies more attractive. In all likelihood, the trend will continue. This creates opportunity for those with capital and vision.

Active, well-capitalised buyers such as Intellectual Ventures (IV), born out of ex-Microsoft and Intel execs, are taking advantage of market inefficiencies and a strong cash position by buying up practically any patents that owners are willing to sell (IV reputedly has more than US$5 billion under management).

Low hanging fruit

At first, IV was able to secure decent rights for a fraction of the R&D, filing and legal fees that went into securing many of them. But with much of the low-hanging fruit already picked, and with the practicality of acquiring invention rights better established, prices are starting to rise. This is likely to benefit strategic investors as much as direct ones, small companies, universities and independent inventors. Currently, IV owns an estimated 15,000 to 18,000 patents that cover a broad range of inventions and technologies. In addition, it has secured scores of patents from its own original filings. How IV plans to monetise these rights remains a mystery. Many are betting that litigation will eventually play a part.

While various types of IP investor are here to stay, the future of IP investing as an industry is less clear. Some of those who invest directly in patents, notably Acacia and Rembrandt, have succeeded in affecting occasional settlements and some damages awards. They all have attracted capital from private equity and other sources; including, in some cases, pension funds and public foundations. None has established a sufficient pattern of ROI to determine its long-term viability.

On the public company side, there are businesses that for strategic reasons use their R&D and patent portfolios primarily to license, not to produce products; such businesses include InterDigital, Rambus, Tessera and Qualcomm. Out-licensing can be an acceptable and prudent business model. Many R&D-based companies have done quite well with a strategy that relies significantly on licensing, but it is unclear whether their successes will endure over time. These entities are under intense pressure to show they can be consistent performers. How well they succeed long term is important, but so is the impact they have had. If nothing else, IP investors with narrower goals have made patent portfolio managers more circumspect about identifying the IP rights and intellectual assets they do not control and deploying those they do.

Bloody footsteps

Operating companies large and small are concentrating more acutely on IP performance. IBM, Intel, HP and GE are all focused on improving their patent portfolios and regularly purge them of unnecessary rights. They are also quietly acquiring and sometimes asserting patents; or at least threatening to. They employ a wide range of techniques to secure, manage, improve and monetise their portfolios.

As a result, a new type of IP investor is emerging. She is less a patent speculator with an eye on out-licensing and assertion than a prudent risk manager willing to place intelligent bets on a variety of relevant internally developed and externally acquired rights. Texas Instruments and other large companies have shown that strategic deployers are not beyond cashing in on their patents directly, engaging in litigation against competitors or even customers. In reality, however, few companies can or wish to follow in their bloody footsteps.

Better measures of patent performance and understanding of their strategic role in product sales, profit margins and competitive advantage will help to relieve some of the pressure on IP managers to seek licensing fees (and engage in litigation) to validate returns. CEOs and Wall Street – I hope you are listening.

Overlooked and understated

2009

The most valuable patents a company owns may not be those that drive licensing deals, but those that underpin products and secure freedom of action.

While IP damages awards and so-called trolls may dominate the headlines, the performance of strategic patents – those associated with managing risk as opposed to generating fees – is generally being overlooked. Effective IAM means different things to different IP holders. One size does not fit every business, nor should it.

Frequently, senior management and shareholders do not recognise their best-performing patents because they protect profit margins rather than generate them.

The problem has a lot to do with identifying the role of a particular patent, or a family of patents, in a given product's success. It also involves the questions: "what is IP performance?" and "what are acceptable methods of measuring it?" For pharmaceutical companies, it is easier to identify successful IP deployment. The Lipitor® patent, for example, probably reads on a single successful product or process and is associated with few, if any, validity issues. In high-tech, there is an ineluctable lack of certainty about most patents' validity, let alone their relevance.

The best strategic patents do their job quietly. They save their owners and licensees huge sums without appearing to do much. What is the value of a patent or family of patents that permit freedom to sell a product unencumbered? To slow a competitor? To facilitate a supply chain or a customer relationship? Often, it is less about what a useful patent generates than what it allows a holder or licensee to retain.

Catalyst for innovation

Non-practising patent owners that speculate on the value of rights and assert them against risk-adverse operating companies, whatever they may be called, can be a catalyst for better innovation. They challenge the most efficient ways for businesses to secure rights and turn inventions into productive assets. They also question the illusion of freedom that piles of irrelevant, uncertain patents imply and many operating companies rely upon. IP investors come in many shapes and sizes, and even those that create pain can serve a purpose. So, too, can patents that prevent disruption or mitigate risk.

The right patents increasingly have been seen as valuable resources, even if they cannot be readily captured and valued like real estate and other tangibles. Not everyone agrees that using patents for direct licensing return and measuring their performance in terms of revenue generated benefits innovation or business objectives. The framers of the US Constitution had unusually high respect for the rights of innovators, such as inventors and authors. While they could not foresee the complex financial engineering that would take place starting in the late 20th century, they did anticipate the impact that rights could have on a broad range of innovative businesses and how that could affect America's competitiveness.

Strategic holders are less sexy. They provide competitive advantage associated with risk avoidance or freedom of action. These advantages are often difficult to identify and quantify. Often, they are more about preventing disruption than creating royalty streams.

Valid and infringed?

Building a portfolio of thousands of patents, as many companies do, is no assurance that they will read on the products that companies sell. In fact, frequently they do not. This leaves operating companies vulnerable to patent suits and damages awards. Some non-practising entities (NPEs) and others attempt to exploit these weaknesses. The question is whether an NPE's patents are valid and actually are infringed. The complexity is compounded by USPTO pendency: it can take as long as five years for some patents to issue and, when they do, they are often of dubious reliability. Patent examination cost, manpower and other issues are factors.

The value of a patent may diminish significantly or even disappear by the time the invention it has been filed to protect is commercialised and goes to market. Indeed, the claims contained in a patent filed on the original invention may differ from those necessary to protect the product actually sold. This can leave conscientious companies vulnerable and frustrated. A wise business needs to keep its perspective regarding not only what IP coverage it has secured through patent filing and in-licences, but which ones it may need but does not have. Good companies do not bury their heads in the sand.

Contentious debate

Patent litigation investors, for example, have effected some attractive settlements and awards. However, it is unclear whether they are of sufficient frequency to compete with the ROI that strategic users generate discretely by attaining freedom of action or standards setting. Better performance metrics will help to sort things out for non-IP professionals.

Patent licensing can be an acceptable and prudent business model for some. Many R&D-based companies have done quite well with a strategy that relies partly or entirely on licensing income, but it is unclear how their successes will endure. If nothing else, IP holders that rely on licensing fees or damages as their primary goals have made patent portfolio managers more circumspect about the need to identify and secure IP rights that they do and do not own. Will alternative models for understanding return on innovation become more ubiquitous as businesses learn to better measure the true financial impact of patents? Time will tell.

Yours, mine, ours

2009

A new book claims that strong patent-holder rights undermine social and business objectives, and waste valuable resources.

How much ownership is "too much" is the focus of a new book, *The Gridlock Economy – How Too Much Ownership Wrecks Markets, Stops Innovation and Costs Lives* (Basic Books).

Written by Columbia University law professor Michael Heller, The Gridlock Economy argues that strong invention rights have reached a point of diminishing returns. Rather than support solutions, Heller believes that patents frequently undermine some companies' ability to provide them. In what he says has become the "anti-commons", IP rights are a burden; a thicket of often ill-granted exclusivity that serious innovators must contend with.

The book describes how inventors' urge to cash in on their proprietary rights is causing companies to abandon commercialising products that can have a positive impact, including those that save lives. Drug makers, says the author, are dissuaded by the veritable minefield of patents they need to negotiate to succeed.

"Imagine twenty or two hundred owners," writes Heller. "If any one blocks the other, the resource is wasted. That's gridlock writ large – a hidden tragedy of the anti-commons." Hidden, he says, because "under use is hard to spot" and because "innovators don't advertise the projects they abandon". Illegal tolls, he asserts, discourage travellers from making the journey. A research director at a pharmaceutical company is cited as someone who "could not figure out how to pay off all the patent owners and still have a good chance of earning a profit".

Drowning in good ideas

The Gridlock Economy suggests that parties are often unable to solve rights disputes and that laws need to be made less tolerant of poor quality. The book is strong on assumptions about what is wrong with patents and their owners, and how they can be fixed by "tuning up" regulations.

It is weak on how businesses can and do coexist and parties successfully compete. While negotiating a thicket of rights can be daunting, cooler heads frequently prevail and most solutions get to market in a timely manner. Remicade is a good example.

In 2004 alone, Johnson & Johnson's anti-inflammatory used to treat rheumatoid arthritis generated US$109 million in patent royalties for New York University (NYU) on revenues of US$2.15 billion. Those figures are up substantially since then. To hedge risk, NYU sold the future royalties of Remicade in 2007 for US$650 million. My understanding is that some 25 other licensors, many of them universities and smaller companies, are benefiting fractionally from developments associated with the drug.

I agree with Heller's main premise that patents can serve as potential barriers to delivering necessary products. However, the book does not distinguish clearly enough between specific contributions, types of owner or industries. Who gets to decide which advances are more important than others? Sometimes what appears to be a minor contribution can be the key that unlocks a successful discovery. The IP executives and attorneys I spoke to think *The Gridlock Economy* may be overstating the case for the commons and understating the case for how the value of complex products can be more fairly divided. Accustomed to playing on a less level field, larger patent holders today are finding they must now accommodate multiple ownership interests to score with new products. This can be maddening for a business under pressure from shareholders or from long-suffering patients and their families.

The contributions of some developments are better understood today than a decade or two ago when, for example, patents were routinely and broadly granted on partial gene discoveries, potentially endangering research. Recently, the Association of Molecular Pathology (AMP) urged an end to granting patents on single genes, sequences of genome or correlations between genetic variations and biological states.

It is not only with life sciences that Heller, a real estate specialist well versed in intellectual property law, has a bone to pick. He believes that similar road blocks exist in property of all sorts. Eminent domain, when a government seizes real estate on behalf of a common good, may work with real estate. In the intellectual property it is interpreted as compulsory licensing and challenges the essence of invention. It is sometimes viewed as a licence to steal.

A two-way street

In a complex world with more rights, less time and increased competition, less clutter can sometimes provide greater benefits. But patent quality and value are context dependent. Increased open innovation is being promoted by many high-tech companies, including IBM and Microsoft. They are not suggesting charitable intent; they seek alternative models to monetise complex investments and generate new business streams. More tech and science companies are working together to set standards and share profits because it can make sense. But for collaboration to succeed, it must be a two-way street.

Don't expect easy answers to complex problems. The argument deftly framed in *The Gridlock Economy* is also timely. Incentive may be the wellspring of invention, but greed, contrary to what Gordon Gekko said in Wall Street, is not necessarily good. The book holds that innovation and its powerful rights are depletable resources that need to be managed responsibly for both investment and social return. Music rights collectives such as ASCAP have successfully negotiated broad copyright use agreements for a variety of composers, musicians and their works. It remains to be seen how many and which patent holders will find such arrangements acceptable.

Don't worry, be happy…

2009

Why it makes sense to bet on IP now.

New York, March 2009 … It's been a long, cold winter. The weather has been frigid and the economic indicators bleak. And there seems to be no end to the rolling tsunami created by the sub-prime crisis. Everyone is paying the cost for false assumptions made about asset quality.

A bright spot amid the gloom can be found in intellectual assets. What is so great about patents and other IP now? Why should businesses and investors think more about licensing, enforcing or acquiring them as the tangible part of the economy dissolves?

For all of their uncertainty, patents offer something of a safe haven from the esoteric financial engineering that got us into this mess. Invention rights, the right ones at least, are attractive investments because of their inherent difficulty, not despite it. It is widely accepted that patents are too easy to obtain, difficult to understand and costly to enforce. Patent holders readily accept those assumptions.

The difference between IP assets and structured finance is that smart people made bad assumptions about questionable debt, like CMOs, but are more sanguine about the meaning of IP rights. Uncertainty makes patents less attractive to some, more to others. Intellectual Ventures reports that of its some 24,000 acquired patents, the average purchase price is still only about US$60,000, up from about US$40,000 a few years ago.

Won't overpay

Patent valuations are moving targets that require context and experience. As a result, patents are conservatively valued and thinly traded, which is bad for sellers and great for smart buyers. Acquirers are unlikely to overpay for patents or get caught holding assets they cannot resell because they rarely have the opportunity to do so.

This is in stark contrast to the meltdown in global-asset backed securities experienced by many financial institutions. Here assumptions about asset quality and market demand ran rampant until the credit carousel stopped and banks and others actually had to mark to market dubious assets. Patent owners are never so lucky – or is that unlucky? They must live with their decisions.

There are many reasons to celebrate patents as investments. Here are nine:
- **Most IP is misunderstood.** New inventions are abstract. So are the rights that protect them. Scepticism about patents is healthy. It is what financial institutions lacked when they engaged in structured finance. Asset-backed investors blindly outbid each other for bad assets; IP investors seldom overpay for acquisitions.

- **Patents are cheap.** Despite the proliferation of IP aggregators such as RPX, Intellectual Ventures, Rembrandts, Coller and Papst, the market for patents relative to the cost in R&D, prosecution costs and filing fees is relatively cheap. The inefficient market means potential opportunities for intelligent buyers.

- **New products will help businesses emerge from the financial crisis.** Whatever the next wave of prosperity looks like, innovation and the rights that protect it will probably play a key role. The worse the financial crisis is, the more important these assets will prove.

- **Strategic patents play a clearer role in profitability.** The freedom of action they provide can generate higher margins and protect market share without generating a dollar of royalties or damages.

- **Higher R&D costs are causing businesses to rethink business models.** Pharma companies learned in the 1980s that they cannot fill their pipeline with in-house discoveries. To succeed, they must identify the right inventions, knowhow and partnerships at the right price. They need to spend less while doing more. High-tech is just learning this.
  - **Open innovation is fuelling broader, better and more efficient investments.** Open invention means greater return for more types of innovators and businesses, and greater efficiency for established ones. OI is not charity; it is good business and it requires the right patents to succeed.

- **Brand names are better positioned to endure an economic crisis; so are branded patents.** Pepsi, P&G, Kraft and McDonald's are considered among the safest investments in a weak economy. Innovation brands such as IBM, HP and Philips are likely to be seen as safer plays, too.

- **The playing field is leveling.** A more diverse and better-informed worldwide pool of innovators and patent holders encourages new ideas. It has become more difficult to infringe today without being caught. This facilitates more licensing and better alternatives or design-arounds. Roadblocks for some are becoming building blocks for others.

- **Some companies need to monetise to survive.** The courts have made it more difficult, uncertain and costly to license patents and enforce them. Selling a patent can be an attractive alternative to companies without the cash, experience or timeframe to monetise it directly.

A better understanding

When wounded companies need cash, all assets are scrutinised; when companies fail, they often leave good assets behind. In past economic crises IP assets were often overlooked in the rush to liquidate real estate and other tangibles. That is unlikely to be the case today. A better understanding of which IP rights are assets and how they return value will help businesses large and small.

Message in a bottle

2009

When it comes to press coverage of IP activities, even good reporters seldom seem to get it right. That's why most IP executives would rather hide from journalists than speak to them. They don't realise that they need the press more than it needs them.

Opting out of press coverage of IP activities is no longer an option. IP rights are integral to the success of most companies and investors; and, like it or not, IP scrutiny is here to stay. A few smart holders are embracing the need for transparency as an opportunity to convey performance and establish a good IP reputation or brand (yes, there are IP brands). Most holders, however, prefer to fly beneath the radar, regarding patents as documents and their strategy, assuming they have one, as a state secret.

Reporters really do strive for accuracy. However, under time constraints, many will file stories whether or not they have had all of the help they need. Good communications start with IP executives providing relevant information in a timely manner. Rather than ruminate about the inherent weaknesses of the press, patent holders should consider taking the initiative by educating reporters about their industry. IP holders also must learn how to become a reliable resource. The burden is on holders of all sizes and business models to provide what every journalist needs: reliable information and context about what it means.

Communication rules

In a recent IAM blog, Joff Wild said that to get the press to take the IP world seriously, IP holders would need to take the press more seriously. He went on to liken journalism (I am paraphrasing) to a competitive sport, where reporters engaged in a constant news battle seek a winning edge. For most IP holders, it is smart to help good reporters do a better job. A first step is being able to help them identify what is real news; the second is to distinguish news from self-promotion.

Journalism is a bit like the law. While there are accepted rules and prescribed behaviours, many areas are left open to interpretation. Reporters need to learn more about IP, what makes it tick and how it impacts on stakeholders. But so, too, do IP owners. Often, it is, as they say, "the blind leading the blind". If IP holders cannot explain their world to corporate executives, they will certainly have a hard time with reporters who maintain higher standards of clarity. IP holders need to learn more about the rules of journalism and what constitutes a good story. I can predict with better than 90% accuracy whether a story will fly or not at a particular publication. No, I am not clairvoyant – just a good listener with better than 20 years of practice.

Help and patience

The business press needs to take IP more seriously and would like to. The IP community, on the other hand, needs to take the business press more seriously and treat its members like professionals. Good IP reporting is not just personality journalism or covering the latest damages award or troll. Innovation rights comprise as much if not more financial value than tangible assets. They help to generate billions of dollars in revenue, affect hundreds of millions of stakeholders and hold the key to the future of both industrialised and developing nations. It is not a matter of whether the business press should cover IP seriously; it is just a matter of when and how.

Unlike tangible assets, patents are difficult to get one's arms around. They are vague and context-dependent, and there are few comparables for pricing them and fewer measures to evaluate their performance. IP rights are a moving target dependent on a myriad of changing legal, business and technical factors. Patents represent inventions that are the product of costly R&D. They enable businesses to innovate, compete; and even, sometimes, collaborate. Companies often cannot live without them, but have a difficult time living with them.

Most journalists can be brought up to speed readily with a little help and patience.

While IP and IP holders may be difficult to cover, so too are subjects such as tax, energy, technology and science, after that, for better or worse, government and the financial markets. Still, somehow, the press does a reasonably good job identifying the necessary facts, assimilating the background and reporting on them in a fair and balanced manner. IP should not be exempt.

Seeking a broader context

Business reporters frequently confide in me that it is difficult to sell an IP story to their skeptical editors. Unless there are significant dollar amounts involved, as in a patent award or settlement, or successful products, colourful personalities or large, widely held public company rights, stories are difficult to put into a broader context. A good reporter's challenge is to be able to identify and frame an IP story in a way that assures accuracy and facilitates relevance. IP holders need reporters to help explain their assets, strategy and performance, and to confer third-party credibility. Companies that say "who cares?" are going to find it difficult to compete in a Facebook cum Twitter universe that requires details be shared quickly and broadly.

Most IP professionals have done an exceedingly poor job of communicating to their constituents and the press the importance of IP. The media in turn has frequently failed to dig below the surface, sticking to clichéd responses: "patents are monopolies"; "those who enforce IP are just out for a quick buck"; worse still, "patents impede innovation". By helping responsible journalists do their job, IP holders help themselves.

More disclosure, less exposure

2009

IP communications is a win-win scenario for most businesses. Holders are starting to realise that sharing some IP information is smarter than hiding all of it.

IP rights confound and confuse. IP communications is a way for patents and other rights to be better understood both inside and outside a business. It paves the way for better performance, higher returns and enhanced shareholder value. Why then are most companies still unwilling to share even the most rudimentary IP information?

Describing intangibles can feel like an exercise in futility. Even those holders who wish to disclose results are uncertain about what and how to. Government regulators, such as the Securities and Exchange Commission in the US, have struggled with how much information investors need to make informed decisions. When it comes to intangibles, such as patents, that comprise the majority of most companies' market value, regulators have steered conspicuously clear.

Why should companies go where regulators have feared to tread? Basically, because it's good business. IP communications (IPC) provides significant advantages to businesses of all sizes and shapes. Moreover, strategic IPC enhances shareholder value and increases positive name (or brand) recognition. With some IP rights, as with shares of equity, the blurred line between perceived value and literal market value can be attributed to reputation. The foundation for establishing brand value is built on reliable information, clearly summarised and consistently delivered. The same is true for intellectual assets.

Hidden opportunity

Sharing IP information should not be seen as a burden or threat. It is an opportunity to convey performance, enhance value, manage risk and, for now at least, steer clear of regulatory scrutiny. Many otherwise intelligent people believe patents are instruments of the devil. Demystifying how a particular business benefits from these exclusive rights helps to counteract the irrational fear they sometimes inspire.

A response that has led many in 2009 to call for an end to patents, which they believe are destroying innovation, or to diminish their impact dramatically through reform legislation. If more companies do not provide some level of IP disclosure soon, I believe that eventually they will be forced to.

Most IP owners are unaware there is a disconnect between them and stakeholders. Securing, deploying and measuring how rights perform affects many outside of the tiny IP orbit. Most holders don't know what assets they own, let alone the best way to discuss them without running afoul of their general counsel or CEO. Many businesses believe that by disclosing less about their patents they can avoid risk; they don't realise how non-disclosure may actually foster it. Without providing IP stakeholders some level of transparency, businesses are in effect saying: "Trust us [you airheads], you don't need to know the big, boring details." In fact, frequently it is the businesses that do not understand the details, let alone how to convey them. This creates a credibility gap between IP holder and stakeholder.

A burden of responsibility

In my last column ("Message in a bottle", IAM 36, June/July 2009), I looked at how the press has been blamed for not understanding IP when holders have done a poor job of helping inform them about what their assets mean and how they are used.

For now, at least, the burden is on the chief IP counsel or business executive to define and manage IP communications.

They need to educate key IP audiences, especially senior management and the media. A few significant IP holders and managers have stepped up and risen to the challenge. IBM, Qualcomm, P&G, Microsoft and Philips come to mind. More are needed. Some may require assistance along the way; all will need to secure the attention and respect of senior management and Wall Street. The IP counsel I speak to believe that data such as patent-related income, freedom of action, and some out, in and cross-licences can be shared without damaging competitive advantage. Best IP disclosure practices should not be confused with identifying cool inventions or supplying global patent counts. Holders must be willing to engage with stakeholders in a meaningful dialogue about what patent quality is and provide contexts for what IP performance means. They also must learn to trust each other. A discussion of IP results and data points quantifying results is not the same as shining a spotlight on innovative new products or inventors.

By whom and to whom?

Many patent attorneys are focused on prosecution. They are not typically equipped to explain IP strengths. Chief patent counsel are often seen as gatekeepers – risk adverse and legal-centric. Good patent litigators, on the other hand, are adept at bringing jurors up to speed about complex inventions and processes. It would be wonderful to apply some of their communications skills to educating clients – and their clients' clients – about IP. In some cases specialised communications or media training may be necessary. And, yes, an IP spokesperson could be a well-informed

C-level executive or business manager.

We need significant IP holders and their managements to disclose clearly and consistently, not just when they have good news to tell. They need to report on changes in IP position in a timely manner, as if the information shared was required. Eventually it will be. The right amount of communication will vary among industries and companies. But disclosures of performance basics such as selected freedom-of-action, licensing and brokerage activity will go a long way towards building trust and establishing an enduring IP brand.

Penny wise, patent foolish

2009

Businesses adept at generating inventions from R&D frequently fail to recognise outside patent opportunities. Who or what is to blame?

"Millions for defense but not one cent for tribute." That is what a feisty Federalist said in 1790 in response to the French threat to seize American ships. This statement is reminiscent of what is said today by any number of technology giants: "Billions for R&D, millions for legal fees, but not one cent for outside patents."

It is amazing how companies adept at identifying and securing their own invention rights are slow to recognise opportunities to capitalise on others'. The "not invented here" syndrome is a disease that runs rampant in good IT businesses from Japan through Europe and to the US. Companies worldwide share a kind of hubris about having all of the inventions (and rights) necessary to compete. Spending literally billions on R&D and maintaining tens of thousands of patents will tend to do that. So will senior managements that are uninformed about how the business of innovation actually works and which executives are really doing their job.

Navel gazing

The mantra for most IT companies goes something like this: (1) we have what we need to practise our inventions; (2) we can always design around a problem, if we have to; and (3) if we do infringe someone will need to catch us and prove it in court. That's costly, time consuming and risky. Besides, if the infringed party is a practising entity, we may be able to neutralise their nastiness with counter-claims on one of their products.

Peter Detkin, co-founder of Intellectual Ventures, tells an illuminating story about patent preparedness. When he was head of patent litigation at Intel in the 1990s he would meet annually with the company's CTO to discuss performance. One year the meeting did not go so well. After an exhausting discussion of costs and returns the CTO turned to Detkin and said: "Your department is the beneficiary of more than US$3 billion in R&D; we also spend well over US$100 million in legal costs and patent filing fees, and you mean to tell me that the company still doesn't have all of the rights it needs to sell its products without interference?" Peter looked up from his spreadsheet and deep into the CTO's eyes. "No," he said. "The products we sell are not necessarily the same ones our patents were intended to cover."

Invention is a complex and iterative process that requires constant adaptation and fine-tuning to make products possible and patents meaningful. As a result, a patent portfolio is not a stagnant bundle of legal rights. It is a living, breathing, changing organism in need of constant nurturing and cultivation. Those relying on an IP portfolio for protection should be as sceptical about the reliability of the coverage it affords as a competitor might be. Few are, and even fewer C-level executives want to think about IP at all.

An ounce of prevention

Most companies have grown to understand that they cannot generate all of the inventions or rights they need to compete. They may indeed conduct huge amounts of expensive research and receive thousands of carefully prosecuted patents, but that does not assure freedom or success. IP-centric companies frequently need to acknowledge, internally, at least, that they likely lack some of the patents they need. Confronting this reality is more daunting to some than others. The solution may require a business to in-license, cross-license or buy patents; and it also may need to purchase whole companies under the right terms. Adapting to the marketplace is often smarter than attempting to satisfy all of a company's innovation needs independently.

Companies as diverse as P&G, Microsoft and IBM all rely on in and cross-licensing to bolster their businesses. So why then do companies which spend so many billions annually on R&D refuse to reserve, say, US$50 million for acquiring patents they need or may require down the road? I think this paradox may have more to do with ego and job security than budget. It also has something to do with the fear of letting competitors see where a business may be weak.

Former MCI and Silicon Graphics chief IP counsel Tim Casey once told me that at a certain stage in MCI's development it was a lot more cost-effective for the telecom company to in-license good patents at the right price covering inventions they definitely use than to come up with the costly alternatives or gamble about not getting caught stealing. Safe passage is costly to procure. However, it is an investment in the future that few companies can afford to ignore.

Embrace opportunity

A better connected and informed – or flatter – world makes it more difficult to infringe competitors' inventions. It also makes it easier and frequently more efficient to acquire innovation from diverse sources. No matter how astutely a company deploys its R&D and its legal resources, it can never be sure if the patents it secures are going to read on the products it actually sells. Often they do not. The emerging marketplace for invention rights provides an opportunity to hedge that risk and improve their IP position. Embracing opportunity is not the same as admitting defeat – GCs and CTOs take note.

A curious journey

2010

After six years and 38 columns "IP investor" emerges with a new name and broader outlook. What does stock investing have to do with patents? Keep reading to find out.

When editor Joff Wild asked me if I would write a column about IP investing for his new magazine, IAM, I wasn't sure if there would be enough material for more than a few issues. It was 2001 and Joff, who had edited my first book, *Hidden Value*, wanted to bring out an IP business publication. This was before anyone knew what NPE meant and when a "troll" was still an ugly little doll.

My involvement with IP began in 1989 when Kenyon & Kenyon, still smarting from a billion-dollar defeat in *Polaroid v Kodak*, retained my firm, Brody Berman Associates, to help rebuild its reputation. We knew about Wall Street from having marketed debt and equity research for financial institutions and from providing shareholder communications to companies like Marvel Entertainment and Autodesk. Joff and I agreed that IP investors were too narrowly defined and that their concerns, including return on costly R&D, needed to be discussed more openly.

Well, 38 columns and some 40,000 words later and I feel like I'm starting to get it regarding the complex role that IP rights play in return on innovation. Their success as investments, I have learned, like stocks, frequently has as much to do with perception as performance. While IP licensing cash flows have been modeled and occasionally securitised, many aspects of IP performance still are not well understood, let alone reflected on balance sheets or income statements, and they may never be.

From frames to claims

My IP journey has been a curious one. Thirty years ago I was a young scholar teaching film studies at Columbia University. My output included structural deconstructions of French New Wave films and DW Griffith shorts. How I traded contemplating frames for claims was mostly an accident. However, the transition seems less surprising to me today than 10 years ago. Visual analysis of moving images and patent management have much in common: both are young disciplines with little history; both lack a common vocabulary; and despite their abundant detail, pictures and patents can be extraoridnarily vague: the more information they provide, the less you seem to know.

This is where investment theory can be useful. Benjamin Graham, an economist who joined the Columbia University Business School faculty in 1928, was an uncharacteristically patient investor and beloved teacher. He believed that the herd mentality should be resisted at all costs. Market swings and over-reactions to shares are merely an opportunity for the Intelligent Investor, the title of his widely read 1949 book.

Margin of safety

Graham, the father of modern investment theory, recommended that investors spend time and effort to analyse the financial state of companies. He believed that when a company's shares are available on the market at a price which is at a discount to their intrinsic value, a "margin of safety" exists which makes them more suitable for investment. The same could be said for intangible assets such as patents, which have less well-defined fundamentals than businesses and securities.

London-born Graham wrote that investment is "most intelligent when it is most businesslike". Many successful investors regard his words as gospel, including Warren Buffet, who named his son for his business school professor. Graham said that the stock investor is neither right nor wrong because others have agreed or disagreed with him; he is right because his facts and analysis are right. The intelligent investor should profit from market folly rather than participate in it. Graham was terrific at marrying theory with practice. His 1934 Security Analysis, which he wrote with David Dodd, is still essential reading in business schools.

IP investors can learn discipline and focus from portfolio theory that emphasizes risk management over speculation. Value investing draws upon fundamentals and looks at multiple factors such as price to earnings ratios, which until the 1930s had little meaning for most investors.

New fundamentals

Investment theory will not generate higher returns for all IP holders. However, I am willing to say that a disciplined, systematic approach to investing in intangibles such as patents, reflective of that practised by Graham and his disciples on stocks, will lead to a sounder methodology. Intellectual assets have more variables to contend with than tangibles. But the amount of capital, cost and value associated with intangibles, including inventions, content, brands and trade secrets, constitute an abundance of wealth that cannot be ignored. IP assets have fundamentals just like operating businesses. It is up to conscientious IP stakeholders to learn what they are and how best to regard them.

It is with intelligent investing in mind and intellectual property the focus that this column will now be called "The intangible investor". The title is not only a play on the title of Graham's enduring book, but a reminder that while innovation rights can be assets, frequently their impact cannot be readily discerned. Consensus on the language and metrics of IP, especially patents, will help to make intangible investing more palpable. Readers of this column tell me that IP accountability is on the rise, especially ROI. I suspect that the good professor is looking down from on high, watching us feel our way.

Far from being an ideologue, Graham wrote that he wished every day to do something foolish, something creative and something generous. Warren Buffett says that Graham excelled most at the last.

What goes around comes around

2010

Half-baked press coverage of IP activities devalues patents and impedes innovation. Blame both reporters and patent holders for not knowing the facts.

Unreliable press coverage of intellectual property developments has become an unsettling fact of business life. It fails in part because fearful patent and other IP holders disclose little and explain less. Reporters get stories wrong because they are confused about the facts and are fed half-truths by IP managers unable to see beyond their immediate focus. That almost no one notices does not make it right.

IP holders quick to point fingers should be prepared to share the blame. Failure to educate reporters about IP is part of the problem; so is the inability to provide basic information about IP performance, such as what it is and how it has an impact on profits.

Members of the business and technology press are as perplexed by innovation rights as IP professionals. They believe what they hear from their sources and have no one to provide a reality check. Too often, they accept myth as fact. IP coverage today still mostly consists of public patent disputes and significant damages awards, among the few vague public disclosures that companies must make. Stories tend to be assigned to a hodgepodge of wary legal, technology and business reporters with a smattering of IP knowledge who are reluctant to challenge what they are told.

The result is reductive and frequently damaging accounts of inflated IP assets and greedy holders. It is curious that IP stakeholders, especially shareholders, have been slow to recognise the impact of misinformation.

Protection racket

An example of dangerously inaccurate IP coverage can be found in a recent *Forbes* article, "Patent Protection for Sale." Written by long-time Silicon Valley correspondent Lee Gomes, the article takes patent aggregator RPX to task for selling protection from lawsuits rather than helping companies, as it claims to. Like other NPEs, says Gomes, RPX merely wishes to profit from others' pain.

A former Wall Street Journal technology specialist, Gomes should know better. He conveys false statements about patent enforcement and a thorough misunderstanding of how IP works. He is probably listening to companies in his own back yard or their advisers. He concludes that RPX's goal is not in fact to help companies but to profit from them (I thought that it is the goal of many businesses to do both?). Gomes writes: "The fact that patent holders and lawyers will end up with money they don't deserve reflects nothing about RPX but a lot about a system filled with rot."

Real inventors

"If you think patents protect plucky inventors and their groundbreaking inventions," Gomes continues, "you haven't been paying attention. Patents have evolved into an extortion scheme that hurts real inventors far more than it helps them."

It sounds like this reporter has swallowed the same concoction that IV's

Peter Detkin did back when he was IP litigation chief at Intel and coined the term "patent trolls". The notion that those who have the audacity to assert their innovation rights or those who might do so on their behalf are somehow less legitimate than "real" inventors whose assignees sell products is not only wrong, it is arguably anti-competitive. Patent quality separates gaming the system for a quick buck from deploying legitimate business assets for maximum ROI.

Gomes states that patent claims (I think he means suits) have soared in recent years: "Roughly 80% are without merit." He says that the figure is a guess provided by RPX, which, by the way, is not now nor ever has been a Brody Berman client. In fact, patent suits have remained basically flat over the past decade, with an average of 2,800 filed annually in the US (they actually dropped by 7% in 2008 and defendants declined by 24%). Despite the headlines, only about 100 suits go to trial annually. This is out of some 185,000 patents awarded on average each year by the USPTO.

"Wouldn't it be nice," concludes Gomes, "if the brainpower involved in an operation like this [RPX] had been used for real innovation?" He misses the point completely. Providing access to valuable rights needed to prevent disputes elevates real innovation; so does holding patent infringers accountable for inventions that they may be stealing. Enforcing patents helps technologies to evolve and new businesses to prosper.
We live in an age of specialisation. Should architects be required to build and sell their buildings to legitimise the originality and ownership of their designs? Should a business or an individual be required to build and sell a product in order to profit from its invention?

Raising the bar

Forbes has a proud history of advocating for business. From the looks of it, the magazine may have lost its way. Suggesting that pro-patent is synonymous with anti-business is irresponsible. This type of lazy reporting affects established businesses and entrepreneurs alike, as well as independent inventors and universities. Accurate coverage starts with IP holders. Journalists need to understand that the IP landscape is complex and dedicated holders are in the position to help.

Those with some IP knowledge or with an agenda are happy to provide whatever facts are convenient for them at a given time. Many are unaware such information can be damaging. Meaningful disclosure helps to counter misinformation; it gives reporters a better shot at doing their job and in turn helps IP professional to do theirs. Patent stakeholders, including investors, who think they may benefit from bad coverage had better watch out. What goes around comes around.

Great expectations

2010

Managing expectations is an important element in establishing patent performance. Who are IP stakeholders and why do businesses need to care about what they think?

Some IP investors are more obvious than others. Those most frequently in the headlines, parties to large patent disputes, such as non-practicsing entities and defendants, represent a fraction of all IP owners and only two of the many audiences affected by IP rights.

For most owners, IP is more associated with risk management and cost savings than direct income streams. Such performance criteria are no less tied to ROI than damages or licensing royalties. Money saved and competitors impeded can have greater value than income earned or value generated.

Those with an interest in IP include stakeholders who may not own patents outright or be invested in businesses that own them. IP stakeholders are customers, vendors, employees and the government, among others. IP stakeholders are better informed than in the past and are more aware of rights as assets. With more audiences than ever affected by the quality and deployment of patents, management ignores stakeholders at its own risk.

Other than direct IP investors, which audiences today have a discernable stake in IP? The boxed-out list on this page is by no means definitive and readers' feedback would be appreciated.

Mindful audiences

Not all audiences mindful of IP performance are necessarily interested in licensing revenue, damages calculations or IP asset sales.

It is difficult today to separate investing in innovative companies (big tech, pharma, VCs) from investing directly in IP rights, such as patents.

With companies now more IP-centric and innovation so costly to procure, maintain and monetise, an equity investment is inevitably an IP one. Audiences such as customers and vendors which benefit from freedom to operate need to rely on IP. Funds that invest in technology or science also must be informed about the quality and performance of IP and IP management.

The emerging interest in innovation rights, in my opinion, has created a unique opportunity for patent holders to evolve from being gatekeepers to information resources. A more inclusive approach to those affected by IP rights, but who may not own them, can be a business asset. And keeping stakeholders reasonably apprised about IP decision-making and performance provides an innovative enterprise with added credibility and transparency.

Investor relations means good communications between principal investors, such as financial institutions and management. However, almost all IR programmes have a significant retail component. Companies know they need to reach out to those individual shareholders and influencers who form important links in their chain of support. Financial reports such as 10Ks and 10Qs may cover a business's legal obligation, but they do not cover its moral one.

Spiderman, too

When Marvel Entertainment was acquired by Carl Icahn from Ron Perelman in 1997 it was in bankruptcy. Following the purchase, it was crucial for Marvel to keep their highly recognisable characters such as Spiderman and Hulk visible, and their loyal fan and investor base informed of what was happening. Marvel knew that if there was to be a future, stakeholders would play an important part. They were right.

Marvel eventually emerged from Chapter 11 and was sold in 2009 to Disney for more than US$4 billion. Treating small investors, employees, vendors, fans and others respectfully made a difference. After a long period in bankruptcy Marvel was still able to generate huge licensing fees on beloved characters; broad shareholder support also was maintained.

It is important for IP holders to remember that performance of their assets affects many different lives. Companies of all sizes that make an effort to explain their intangible assets to those who are affected by them are in a better position to strengthen their supply chain, attract cheaper capital and cement customer relationships. Burned stakeholders (no pun intended) have long memories.

Audiences with an interest in IP performance are as much intangible investors as NPEs; yet managements tend to regard them as invisible – and you do not get more intangible than that.

There are benefits from recognising the interests of IP stakeholders, even if most are not literally investors. Companies that go out of their way to keep them up to date with IP developments and treat them cordially are more likely to manage expectations and minimise disruptions.

Measures of success, too

2010

Former chief IP execs at Microsoft, HP, IBM and Apple were asked to weigh in on patent performance. What they had to say may surprise you.

"What you can't measure, you can't manage," said Peter Drucker, one of the great management strategists and writers.

Intellectual property's greatest challenge revolves around measuring what many believe cannot be reliably counted – patent performance. Patent performance is so frustrating a challenge that otherwise courageous executives avoid doing it or simply say that it cannot be done. IP value means different things to different rights holders at a given point in time. Patents, especially, are informed by quality, or validity, and context. And context is rarely constant.

For some businesses, patent performance is about royalties; for others, freedom to sell a product unencumbered; for still others, it is the ability to mitigate risk. Performance can mean maintaining market share for a particular product, slowing a competitor or enhancing profit margins. Ask 10 IP professionals how patent performance is best measured and you will likely get 20 or more responses.

Rather than speculate about how companies measure patent performance, I asked three successful IP executives who have firsthand experience. How do they gauge success and, more importantly, how did their stake holders? The responses were revealing.

Apple, HP, IBM, Microsoft

All of the interviewed executives worked in the tech sector. Two were heads of IP business units, Joe Beyers at HP and Marshall Phelps at both IBM and Microsoft; and one, Irv Rappaport, was a CIPO with a strong business focus. Rappaport headed patent and trademarks for Apple, National Semiconductor and Medtronic. In 1994 he co-founded the first company to provide software for competitive patent analysis. Bruce Berman: What were the primary ways that patent performance was measured at the IP business units you headed?

Irv Rappaport: The chief criteria at the companies I worked for were litigation avoidance, cross-licences with major competitors, strategic patent rights acquisitions and out-licensing income, pretty much in that order.

Joe Beyers: Litigation avoidance is a difficult metric, as patents are not of much value when faced with an assertion brought by an NPE. In only a few cases can you trade patents to reduce or eliminate assertion risk from them. The performance measures of an IP licensing programme for a company like HP are summarised in "Measuring and Conveying IP Value in the Global Enterprise", my chapter in the book From Assets to Profits [ed Bruce Berman, 2008, John Wiley & Sons].

Patent counts have been waning in significance, as in general the industry is starting to understand better the importance of quality versus quantity. Invention disclosures are an even worse metric. They can be increased easily and artificially to inflate the invention disclosure count by providing excessive incentives.

Marshall Phelps: At IBM, product revenues were the highest priority; so were licensing numbers, especially being number one in patents granted and patent quality.

For Microsoft, numbers of licences are very important. They went from basically no patent licences in the mid-1990s to well over 600 today. Many of these licences are less about generating product revenue than achieving leverage and protecting sales. Being ranked number one in patent quality also is very important to them.

Second-class status

Intangible assets' second-class status is a result of the frustration their performance generates. Bringing order to the chaos of patent performance helps those less informed about the IP, such as c-level executives, capital providers and shareholders, to recognise intangibles as potential financial assets. It also permits those charged with managing and monetising them to plan and secure broader support.

BB: What were some of the techniques you used to explain patent performance internally to non-IP professionals?

IR: We held meetings annually with key executives to explain our overall patent strategies and objectives and what we were doing to meet goals.

JB: It starts with an educational process – with both executives and the general development and business community in a company. At HP, it has been reported publicly that my function created an IP training class that was deployed throughout the company. Educating people about the nature and importance of IP is highly impactful, especially when this is coupled with case study examples of the impact of both ineffective and effective uses of IP.

MP: Everyone understands the importance of revenues, so if you build financial expectations into the business unit plans (or licensing targets or whatever), then you have allies in reaching those targets. If you have the CEO in line with the IP goals and targets, it helps persuade management in general, as well as those lower down in the organisation.

Common themes

The common theme emerging from the discussion about performance is that it differs from company to company, even for those in the same industry. Factors such as size, appetite for risk, invention quality, timing and access to capital influence how patents can be deployed. There are times when pursuing out-licensing income may make terrific sense, and others when the difficulty and disruption of patent enforcement simply do not provide enough return; and money saved is worth more than revenue generated. Generating licensing revenues? A clear win. Translating less obvious patent benefits to the P&L? Priceless.

Measures of success, III

2010

Understanding patents starts with a business's ability to identify needs, establish expectations and measure performance. It's easier said than done, say three experts.

Patent performance means different things to different holders at different points in time. Last month I asked chief IP execs formerly of Apple, Microsoft, HP and IBM how they measured and communicated patent performance. This is the conclusion of that discussion.

Bruce Berman: Freedom to operate is worth more to some companies than licensing income. How difficult is it to translate this to a P&L?

Irving Rappaport: The larger the company, generally, the more important it is to secure freedom and sell products. With some smaller companies, out-licensing income can be a more important component of the company's bottom line. At National Semiconductor, a US$1.7 billion company, we brought in US$250 million in royalties from 1991 to 1993 at a time when all the operating divisions of the company were losing money. Those royalties helped get the company through a very difficult period.

Joe Beyers: Freedom to operate is the highest priority, unless IP licensing is central to the overall business strategy, which is rarely the case. The value of freedom is unfortunately very difficult to quantify.

Imagine needing to trade off an opportunity to obtain $XYZmillion/yr in [highly profitable] licensing revenue against an opportunity to obtain a cross-licence to IP that could be damaging to a core product. A simple analytical model will not suffice. You have to consider factors such as:

- The probability of actually closing the licensing deal and whether the licence for which you are getting across will actually impact on your product/ business.

- The expected future growth/decline in the revenue and profit of the product business.

- The overall impact to the core of the company of having the product line affected – that is, the halo effect to your other lines of business.

- The costs (actual and opportunity) for defending the product or business.

Marshall Phelps: Freedom of action is one positive consequence of a robust patent and licensing programme. Unfortunately, it's not easily translated into a P&L.

For IBM in 1992, out-licensing was more an act of survival than an innovative IP strategy. The company was on the verge of bankruptcy and freedom to sell product was certainly important, but so was generating enough cash flow to remain solvent.

Berman: Many high-tech companies believe that improving their patent portfolio through acquisition, in-licence or sale is like admitting defeat. This would seem counter to IAM best practices.

Rappaport: That's a very narrow view of ROI. If the acquired rights help the company's overall business strategy, it should be seen as a win-win, particularly if it would take a long time for the company to develop its own rights in the acquired technologies. The terms of the deal also are important.

Beyers: Defeat may not be the proper term. It is more like anger that they now have to pay a third party, perhaps a competitor, to execute their business strategy. Compounding the problem is that this cost was likely not forecasted in the financial model/budget. Surprise expenses are the worst kind of costs to an operating company or division.

Phelps: Forward-thinking companies don't believe that in-licensing or patent acquisitions are weaknesses. Despite spending about US$8 billion in R&D, Microsoft went out and bought another US$1.4 billion in patents when it saw fit to do so. It's impossible for most companies to rely solely on the discoveries they make and patents they file. If they can't license-in or cross-license to get what they need, sometimes it makes sense to buy patents at the right price or to join a group like RPX or AST. When IBM needed to generate cash fast, patent and technology licensing seemed to make the most sense. The emergence of the internet was a sort of second chance for IBM, which developed new ways of generating cash flow and being profitable. With Microsoft, IP was not about cash generation. It did not need to be. If anything, it was about revenue preservation and risk management. These are two different companies with different product lines and performance criteria. Both are companies that are high on the range of IP sophistication and make good use of a variety of performance generating tools.

No surprise

It's no surprise that three heads of IP business produced three-plus perspectives on patent performance and measurement. Companies have different IP needs at different points in their evolution. It's nice for an operating company to say: "No thank you. We have all of the IP we need." But that level of self-sufficiency would be rare for most innovation-dependent businesses, ever mindful of R&D costs, filing fees and litigation risk.

Businesses need better systems for recognising the intellectual assets they have and those they do not. They also need to provide senior management with a more relevant IP dashboard.

Would anyone have noticed the genius of RIM settling its patent dispute with NTP for a mere US$35 million to US$50 million early on when it could have?* IP executives and CIPOs tend to get fired for that kind of wise deal making, especially when senior management and BODs are confused about IP in the first place.

Highly abstract IP wins can be more clearly identified and deftly communicated without threatening competitive advantage or increasing levels of anxiety. It's up to responsible IP execs to make sure the story gets told accurately and to the right audiences.

*Research in Motion was forced to settle for $612.5 million.

Patentomics

2010

Proposals to establish a small claims court for patent disputes in the US and to use patents to create jobs hold promise. But the devil is in the details.

Disputes over innovation are inevitable. How they get resolved is not. While well over 95% of American patent suits settle, the cost in time, money and disruption is problematic for both alleged infringer and infringed.

Robert P Greenspoon, a partner at Chicago IP law firm Flachsbart & Greenspoon, LLC, is offering a solution. In "Is the United States Finally Ready for a Patent Small Claims Court", an article he wrote for the *Minnesota Journal of Law, Science & Technology*, he argues that this resolution alternative, similar to binding arbitration, would benefit plaintiff and defendant alike.

"A Patent Small Claims Court would fill [a] gap in our system," says Greenspoon. "… If there were a good, cheap, and fast way to bring a small claim to resolution, the patentee's dilemma would be vastly reduced… A small claims court for patent disputes would help individuals, small businesses, large businesses, and the court system itself.

In contrast to the present patent litigation environment, where individuals or small businesses often cannot economically enforce their intellectual property rights even when they are willfully infringed upon, such a court system would provide a new opportunity. Unblocking access to the courts for a deserving subset of patentees will have the salutary effect of encouraging innovation. Helping innovation, in turn, helps consumers."

False proxy value

The author concludes that large entities would also benefit from a small claims forum because they are most affected by "a certain type of plaintiff who uses the costs of litigation (rather than the merits of the claim) as a false proxy of settlement value".

Greenspoon's analysis is timely. However, his proposal raises unanswered questions. For example, what about patent quality? Inventors may be encouraged to unleash a stream of marginal or even fallacious claims against risk-averse companies because they know that they are likely to be settled quickly. Once patentees are aware that XYZ Tech is paying up to prevent disputes from getting to district court, patent filing could become an end for cash-strapped companies, not the means to create innovation. Defendants that may wish to view these awards as a relatively inexpensive field of use licence certainly could benefit. However, there is no clear indication of what the limits of "small" claims should be: US$1 million? US$100,000? How would validity be established? Or would the alternative court even bother to? Who would be qualified to hear small disputes?

The idea of a small patent claims court is not entirely new. In 1990, a Patents County Court was established in the United Kingdom as an alternative to the High Court for patent litigation. It would be interesting to know how it has fared.

Another proposal, this one to facilitate jobs by encouraging innovation, was offered recently in a *New York Times* editorial, "Inventing Our Way Out of Joblessness". The authors are former Chief Judge for the Court of Appeals for the Federal Circuit Paul Michel, a 2010 IP Hall of Fame inductee, and Henry Northhaft, CEO of Tessera (NASDAQ: TSRA), a successful patent licensing company. Joining them on the op-ed was uncredited collaborator David Kline, co-author of *Rembrandts in the Attic* with Kevin Rivette and *Burning the Ships* with Marshall Phelps.

The trio suggested that attributing more patents to small and medium-sized businesses would spur innovation, which in turn would stimulate the economy by creating jobs – a kind of patentomics.

"Our guess is that restoring the patent office to full functionality would create, over the next three years, at least 675,000 and as many as 2.25 million jobs. Assuming a mid-range figure of 1.5 million, the price would be roughly $660 per job — and that would be 525 times more cost effective than the 2.5 million jobs created by the government's $787 billion stimulus plan."

Increased funding to relieve USPTO backlogs and enhance the quality of issued patents makes great sense. But where the authors' logic eludes me is in their proposal to pay inventors to file patents by providing a cash incentive to cover about half of the cost: "To encourage still more entrepreneurship, Congress should also offer small businesses a tax credit of up to $19,000 for every patent they receive, enabling them to recoup half of the average $38,000 in patent office and lawyers' fees spent to obtain a patent. Cost, after all, is the No. 1 deterrent to patent-seeking, the patent survey found.

"For the average 30,000 patents issued to small businesses each year, a $19,000 innovation tax credit would mean a loss of about $570 million in tax revenue in a year. But if it led to the issuance of even one additional patent per small business, it would create 90,000 to 300,000 jobs."

Change or progress?

More patents are an unreliable indicator of increased innovation. Offering cash incentives to secure them is no guarantee of success. Unless there is a way to monitor the quality of issued patents that result, these rewards may in fact encourage some entrepreneurs to file applications haphazardly or on inventions which do not fully meet the tests of patentability. Also, when would the cash be paid? Upon filing? Upon publication? Upon issuance? Even with a less backlogged PTO, it may be five or more years before the incentives reach those who need them most.

Independent and small business innovation has historically played a key role in US growth. The government needs to be more innovative about how it manages innovation, including disputes. Kudos to Messrs Greenspoon, Michel, Northhaft (and Kline) for suggesting how the patent system can be improved. But, as with patent claims, the devil is in the details. Potential defendants and their stakeholders will need convincing that change means progress.

Agent provocateur

2011

Legendary film director Jean-Luc Godard has declared there is no such thing as intellectual property. Such iconoclasm is something he once great director can afford to promote.

As a lecturer at Columbia University 30 some years ago, I had the pleasure of teaching the French *Nouvelle Vague*, or New Wave, one of the richest periods in film history. Led by Francois Truffaut, Claude Chabrol, Eric Rhomer and Alain Resnais, these 1950s filmmakers successfully challenged Hollywood conventions of narrative and character development. Many of their techniques were eventually adopted by mainstream directors.

The most notorious of these *enfants terribles* was Jean-Luc Godard. Godard is responsible for such influential works as *Breathless, Band of Outsiders* and *Weekend*. These films often included his signature jump cut, a jarring narrative leap that was freely copied, but never quite reproduced. Godard is undisputedly among the most important filmmakers of the past 50 years and possibly in history, and he will receive an honorary Academy Award if he agrees to accept it.

Godard's complex and often challenging films flirt with existentialism, Maoist politics and screwball comedy. They are less politically extreme than intellectually defiant – a kind of literary pop art. His work, rife with references both to modern philosophy and to Hollywood movies, established him as a charming but elusive cineaste, more Bob Dylan than Jean Paul Sartre.

Rights or duties?

All of this is pretext for recent news coverage about the 79-year-old director coming to the aid of known copyright pirate James Climent. After a 2005 search of his hard drive turned up more than 13,000 mp3 files, Climent was ordered to pay more than US$25,000 in damages. Ever defiant, Climent, told Alexandre Hervaud of Ecrans that today he has "more than 30,000 files". He now wants to take his case to the European Court of Human Rights in Strasbourg, and Godard has decided to help him with a little money and a lot of publicity. According to website TorrentFreak, a file-sharing blog, the still active filmmaker recently donated €1,000 to the photographer's legal fund.

"While Mr. Godard's views on intellectual property are widely shared on the libertarian fringes of the internet," stated one news account, "they might seem surprising coming from a director, who under French law, retains editorial control over his work and derives financial benefit from it."

Apparently, Godard still delights in pushing the boundaries. When it comes to IP rights on the internet, some music fans prefer to believe the Hollywood-inspired myth that pirates such as Climent are actually folk heroes, and those who seek to protect innovators and their works from being copied without their permission are merely dull defenders of the state. Unfortunately, the belief makes for the better story than the truth.

File-sharing debate

In an interview in the French cultural magazine *Inrockuptibles*, Godard said: "There is no such thing as intellectual property... Copyright really isn't feasible. An author has no rights. I have no rights.

I have only duties." Perhaps if Godard, once a publicist for Twentieth Century Fox in Paris, were as impassioned about the rights to his own *oeuvre*, he would have turned down, or at least donated, some of the royalties they generated. (A link to the translation of the entire interview with him can be found on *IP Insider*.)

Godard's controversial move comes as the debate in France over file sharing is growing more contentious. At about the same time as the director announced his support for file sharing, Google Inc's YouTube struck a deal with France's biggest music rights body to pay composers when their songs are viewed. Under the agreement, SACEM, the French society for authors, composers and music publishers, will collect, receive and distribute royalties to its members based on the number of times their songs are viewed.

Meanwhile, the government of French President Nicolas Sarkozy is seeking tougher measures to strengthen IP laws, which have been fiercely contested by the Socialists, who are normally aligned with the cultural establishment. The centrepiece of Sarkozy's piracy crackdown is the so-called graduated response law, under which people who share digital songs, films or other media content could face the suspension of their internet connection if they ignore repeated warnings to quit.

Attracting attention

Somewhere between absolutely no file sharing, the authorised distribution of music (e.g. iTunes), and making all digital content available without cost to anyone with a PC lies a workable system. Those who advocate free exchange have little to say about how less famous musicians and other artists, such as photographers, can be supported. While money may not be everything to them, many still depend on the web for at least a part of their income, and it beats working as a cashier in the supermarket. Unauthorised file sharing, while useful to a few artists' careers, will probably destroy many others'.

Enforcing IP rights does not seem very stylish, but without restrictions on access to innovation, there would be fewer recordings worthy of Climent's bulging hard drive. Artists and innovators can be compelling, even disruptive, without forsaking their proprietary rights. Not all of them are in the position to be generous with their work or, as with savvy performers like Prince, to bypass record labels and turn inevitable poaching into direct consumer marketing.

Godard, more a *provocateur* than a politician and with a new film about to come out, is making a vague if convoluted point about controlling the dissemination of creative ideas. If the storylines of his films are any indication, Godard's attraction to dreamy, self-styled culture heroes like Climent has not diminished. Nor has his penchant for stirring the pot.

Bloggers 1, business press 0

2011

The business media are doing a better job of covering patent disputes. However, they still have a long way to go if intellectual property is to be taken seriously by non-IP audiences.

Publications such as the *Financial Times*, the *Wall Street Journal* and *Bloomberg BusinessWeek* have become increasingly aware of the impact of IP rights. Unfortunately, they may not realise that covering complex and costly patent disputes requires IP perspective as well as journalistic skills.

Most people believe that regarding patents is akin to watching paint dry. Journalists are not much different. The result is that when they report on developments, they may rely too much on what their sources tell them is important, as opposed to determining what really is. It's puzzling to me that otherwise reliable financial news sources often refuse to assign reporters to a regular IP beat.

IP press coverage over the past 20 years has been primarily confined to disputes involving large public companies, significant damages awards and non-practising entities, still often reduced to trolls. A handful of blogs, notably Gene Quinn's *IP Watchdog*, the *IAM* blog, Dennis Crouch's *PatentlyO* and my *IP Insider*, are treading where the mainstream business media typically fear to.

The best blogs attempt to unbundle the issues and sort the facts, where much of the mainstream press is looking at them in broad brush strokes. It's ironic that it has fallen to a handful of legal or tech reporters, few with patent exposure, and a coterie of jaded if dedicated part-time writers to provide perspective about developments that collectively affect tens of millions of people and billions in market value.

Rising interest

Interest in IP transactions, too, is starting to attract media attention. For example, Bankrupt Canadian network company Nortel's 4,000 patent portfolio is expected to generate US$1 billion for creditors. While Apple and Google don't appear to need the patents today to sell their products, they reputedly want them to bolster their portfolios, and possibly to use the patents as dry powder against those networking companies that do. Reuters did an excellent job of explaining the build-up to the private auction.

In fairness, it is not easy to get IP holders to talk about their intentions. For many patent holders, the less people know, the better. This is likely to change as affected parties ask more difficult questions, and publicly held operating companies must learn to manage their IP transparency.

In a recent *Forbes* article, "Going Toe to Toe with Medical Device Giants", the magazine does a credible job of conveying a complex patent dispute involving designer Nova Biomedical, but fails to explain that the business of patent defence is often a more significant problem for large companies than smaller ones. The article details how tiny Nova prevailed against Abbott, Roche and Medtronic regarding the rights to a glucose meter for diabetics. The piece is undermined by over-relying on its resources.

Ropes & Gray describes how difficult it is for players such as Nova to go up against larger competitors that want to bury them. At one point, Nova defended itself against three separate suits which it eventually had to secure loans to finance. The apparent take-away: patent litigation is more expensive for some defendants than others; important cases need large law firms.

Hung out to dry

It is no surprise that legal battles involving inventions are expensive. Still, the article underestimates the cost. Early on, Nova chose to collaborate with insulin syringe maker Becton Dickinson, which was eager to get into a new product line. Unfortunately, it picked the wrong partner. Becton Dickinson required Nova to cover any potential litigation costs and, when the going got tough, pulled the plug on its nascent glucose monitoring business, leaving Nova without a partner.

Why wouldn't competitors move in for the kill if they could? Perhaps Nova's patent portfolio was not as robust as it had thought and cutting a licensing deal with its adversaries less of an option. The *Forbes* story was curiously bereft of this scepticism. It compiled data from several sources, including Ropes, PwC, Stamford and the USPTO for a sidebar that attempts to illustrate the high costs associated with patent disputes. These facts tell only part of the story. (My addenda in italics.)

Pricey patents

US$10 million – cost to defend a high-stakes patent suit.
The average patent suit today costs US$5 million-plus. Significant disputes that go to trial can exceed US$100 million, and it is not unusual for a plaintiff's legal fees to run to US$20 million or US$30 million, depending on the amount of potential damages involved.

US$3.8 million – median damages awarded in patent infringement cases from 2001-07
Most defendants' main worry is large patent awards, which can exceed $1b (Karlin v Medtronic, US$1.4 billion; J&J v Abbott, US$1.7 billion), and settlements that can be similarly high (NTP v RIM, US$612 million). While eBay v MerchExchange

may have made them less automatic, the threat of an injunction is still one of a plaintiff's most potent weapons.

2,700 – Average number of patent-infringement lawsuits filed per year
The average number of patent infringement suits is only about 1.4% of the patents issued annually. They are less rampant than the media would have us believe. Eighty six percent settle before trial (Professor Paul Janicke, Universtiy of Houston).

100 – Average number of patent cases that go to trial each year
Despite the headlines about disputes and worldwide increases in innovation, US patent trials have remained virtually flat for 20 years. The percentage of patent suits that go to trial (3.7%) has actually decreased. The number of defendants may in fact be up.

An image is worth 10,000 words

2011

Businesses that have a reputation for successfully identifying and managing IP rights could be sitting on an overlooked asset – their patent brand.

What's in a name? Apparently a great deal when it comes to facilitating higher return on rights such as patents.

A reputation for success is gravitational. Audiences are drawn to iconic businesses, universities and personalities like a moth to light. Reputation simplifies matters and satisfies the psyche. It renders impressions more manageable and decision making less arduous. In a digital universe, with far too much information to process, less can be much more. Audiences would prefer to accept that a+b+c = x, as long as x is generally reliable over time.

If a picture is worth 1,000 words, then when it comes to patents, which can be dizzyingly complex, a positive image is worth 10,000.

A global 500 IT company recently retained my firm, Brody Berman Associates, to explore which patent holders are seen as the leading players. The client wanted to learn on what the responding IP executives based their conclusions. The client was also interested to discover (anonymously) how it ranked. The findings of the relatively small sample, while hardly definitive, shed light on how IP opinions are formed.

On matters such as the relative importance of patent counts, the respondents agreed strongly; on others, they were divided. All had strong opinions about which patent holders were exceedingly good at identifying and managing IP within their respective industries, even if the conclusions were frequently based more on impression than fact.

The findings suggest that licensing income is a more important indicator of success to some than others. Non-IP people, such as chief executives and investors, are better able to process the meaning of revenue. The respondents agreed that patent counts were highly overrated and meant more to a general business audience than to those who made their living from IP. Risk mitigation was the least obvious and most difficult measure of strength, yet for large operating companies it was probably the most relevant.

Businesses such as IBM, Microsoft, Qualcomm and Philips were more highly regarded by survey respondents, not only because IP rights play a role in their success, but because these companies remind audiences that they do. There was the widest disagreement about Cisco. Perception of its IP performance differed broadly. Some thought it smart of it not to rely too heavily on patents and to settle disputes; others thought Cisco shortsighted for not having a more reliable portfolio.

The survey take-away: a lack of information about a company's patent performance relative to its industry is at best confusing and at worst damaging. The professionals' take on whether a business's patent strategy and rights were meaningful, while often accurate, tended to be based more on impression than on fact.

Accessing patent performance can be daunting. A reputation for extracting value from patents enables diverse IP audiences – these days pretty much everyone from shareholders to customers to employees – to have a handle on results. While companies can and do conduct their IP business in the dark with little consequence, results that are conveyed strategically over time can turn a solid reputation into a brand.

Understanding the role of patents in a particular transaction or business objective is not as simple as adding spreadsheet columns A, B and C. Many elements go into providing an accurate representation of performance. Most managements believe either that IP results cannot be explained or that no one of consequence is listening.

If that were true, it is less so today, as the importance of IP increases and the audiences affected by it are better informed.

What constitutes an IP reputation is really no different from what goes into any positive business profile: clarity, credibility, consistency – words that are more easily spoken than embodied.

Some companies with a strong consumer brand are in a position to help their patents. P&G, with well over 20,000 worldwide patents and the stated desire to license any of them after three years, has leveraged its formidable brand equity on behalf of its patent portfolio. Others known primarily for their technology innovations (eg, Micron) may have to work harder to establish their innovation reputation. Patent brand holders are more likely to enjoy better values, more favourable transaction terms and higher stock price. They may also find greater customer support and stronger, more loyal vendor relationships.

While the value of patent prowess is difficult to quantify in absolute terms, IP reputation management is something that IP Hall of Fame executives such as Marshall Phelps (Microsoft, IBM) and Ruud Peters (Philips) have been practising for years. They know that it pays.

At its best, image provides an aura of success that, while based on literal performance, in the end transcends it. What makes Goldman Sachs *Goldman* is not an accident. It is a generally accurate depiction of what the company has achieved in finance and the values it stands for. The image is based on fact, but emboldened by reputation. When questionable practices threatened that profile during the financial crises, the Goldman brand was tarnished and its margins threatened. I am certain that the company will work quickly to restore the lost lustre.

The problem with a brand is that, once established, it cannot be taken for granted; it needs to be continually nurtured. Yes, those companies with a reputation for identifying and managing patents are in a better position to benefit when they succeed. They also are in a position to be adversely affected when they fail to meet expectations.

Like consumers, IP stakeholders have long memories and trust that is violated can turn a brand against itself. Just ask GM or Chrysler.

Cash: patents' once and future king

2011

Equity investors are hot for the profit potential of patents. Some IP holders are hoping that cooler heads will prevail.

Wall Street's love-hate relationship with IP rights is heating up. It's in the interest of IP holders to make certain cool heads prevail.

A JP Morgan report on Acacia Technologies (NASDAQ: ACTG), a patent licensing company that barely survived 2003, sheds light on the strengths and weakness of public licensing. By racking up a critical mass of patent settlements and a few forward-looking licences, Acacia has caught the attention of mainstream investors. With the help of Barclays Capital (RPX co-underwriter), the company recently raised another US$175 million in a stock offering. As of press time, it enjoys a US$1.5 billion market valuation.

In an industry that prides itself on the ability to discount almost any type of risk, Wall Street finds IP-centric companies such as IBM interesting; those that license patent rights as their primary source of income, it finds tantalising. The difference is in the financials – especially operating margins, which can be double or higher than those of the average S&P 500 company. Wall Street is also turned on by the explosive growth of

Acacia, which for now, appears to have established a sufficient pipeline of deals to smooth any significant lumps in its earnings.

Is Wall Street ready to accept the patent licensing business for what it is? Are companies that license for a living sufficiently scalable (and sustainable) for institutional investors, pension funds and the like? Probably, yes.

In recent years a number of companies established primarily for patent income have come and gone. Several were publicly held or tried to go public, hoping to avail themselves of the capital markets. The transparency required for public ownership is less at odds with how an IP licensing businesses operates than at first glance. Disclosure can facilitate good IP practices by demystifying the process and may also encourage the timely resolution of disputes to satisfy earnings expectations.

Acacia seems to have broken the threshold for patent licensors. It has provided apparent financial legitimacy to a business model of which many investors remain sceptical. Acacia's ability to source and settle disputes involving infringed patents which it co-owns as opposed to purchases has taken it far. Some believe that it settles enforcement actions expeditiously because many of its patents are not trial-worthy. It has spent barely US$10 million annually over the past three years to acquire licensing enforcement opportunities, which JP Morgan rightly finds unsustainable. In contrast, Intellectual Ventures has spent US$2 billion or more on its 30,000 patent portfolio.

A recent 44-page equity report by JP Morgan analyst Paul Coster provides a detailed look at Acacia's finances, prospects and the future of the patent licensing industry. It is an excellent report, clearly written and thoughtfully researched, no doubt with some guidance from Acacia executives. Coster makes a strong case for patent licensing, suggesting as I and others have for the past decade that a more orderly market for resolving patent disputes provides greater transparency and liquidity to a market that is desperately in need of it. Acacia is a means to an end for operating companies, wary of uncertainty.

According to Coster, Acacia's 50% gross profits and 30% operating margins should improve even further. He observes that "corporations and their patent attorneys recognize Acacia's role in the market and often chose to default licensing negotiations". He expects about 23% revenue growth over the next three years. FY 2011 earnings per share are estimated at US$0.98, against a loss of US$0.38 in 2010.

Some industry watchers believe that Acacia settles early and grabs the cash. In fairness, that it sues first and negotiates later is at least in part a response to the threat of declaratory judgment, which unfortunately is becoming the norm among IT defendants. A licensing business that earns a reputation for settling disputes and generating a reasonable return from a volume of transactions, rather than relying on a few big ones, may be a more workable model than more focused patent enforcement firms such as Rembrandt are willing to admit.

Fast-track market licences may be are a reasonable alternative to compulsory licences and all-out litigation war that costs everyone. That this business model may strike fear in the hearts of some law firms is no surprise. Acacia is the leading litigant among non-practising entities, responsible for 10% of the suits. Whatever the reason, it has done a good job of avoiding the highest-cost litigation. Can Acacia eventually serve as a kind of ASCAP of invention rights, a clearing house that provides what parties are willing to live with as opposed to what they demand?

The keys for Acacia as I see them: maintaining patent quality; the need to win big in court every now and then to show licensees it is capable of doing so; and the ability to license on behalf of at least some large operating companies, not just to them.

I have been preaching for the past 10 years that patent holders need to do a better job of explaining and qualifying their wins. For most, their success has more to do with mitigating risk or assuring sales freedom than generating cash flow. In the end, it is about achieving business goals. Acacia's success, unfortunately, encourages Wall Street to focus on direct revenue and obscures the value of strategic patents. Hopefully, that fixation is temporary.

Patent licensing has become something of a symbiotic industry – Acacia is dependent to an extent on RPX's and AST's success, as well as IV's, InterDigital's and others'. They all rely on the high cost of litigation. These patent holders feed off each other by offering diverse solutions to a similar problem. They all need the respect and participation of operating companies to succeed.

Together, these strange bedfellows are conjuring the future of innovation and, for now at least, have caught Wall Street's roving eye.

Model behaviour, redux

2011

Diverse businesses have made monetising patents more lucrative and less painful. They have come a long way, but are yet to be fully understood.

Civilisation required more than two million years to evolve from the Palaeolithic or Old Stone Age and the use of crude tools to the beginnings of the pre-industrial Bronze Age. It has taken the patent ecosystem about a decade to establish the foundation of its future.

IP humans are working with better tools, but they are also doing what they do best: using their imagination. Peter Holden, head of IP Investments at Coller Capital, recently came to me with a graph which illustrates the IP acquisition marketplace. Peter asked me to review the approach and otherwise challenge the assumptions before he went public with it. The result appears in "New models in response to changes in the global IP market" (*IAM* issue 48).

The acquisition marketplace looks at the amount and nature of key players' funding. What the survey chose not to cover at that time are the number and source of their patents (ie, whether they originate internally or are acquired, or both), and the extent to which litigation plays a role in strategy. Brody Berman Associates fleshed out this alternate view in conjunction with Coller. We call it the patent monetisation landscape.

(The graph is not drawn to exact scale and excludes operating companies.)

Figure 1. **The patent monetisation landscape**

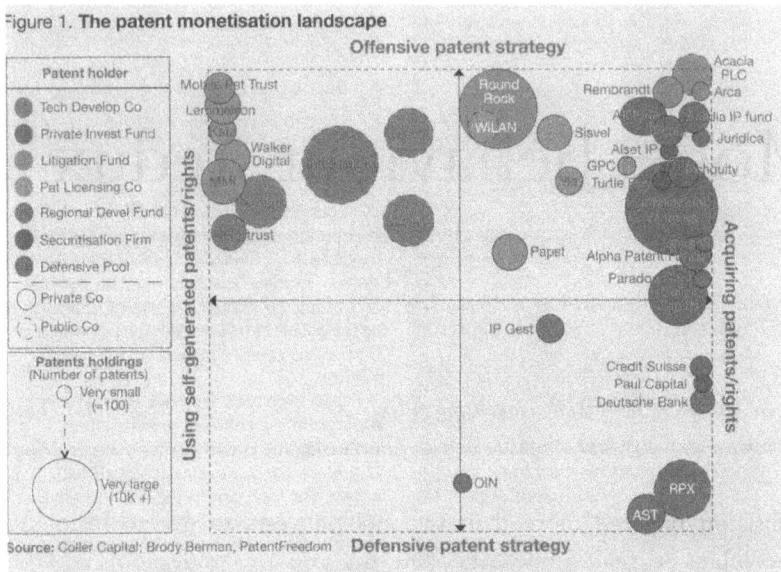

Source: Coller Capital; Brody Berman, PatentFreedom

The result provides insight into how far IP management has come and the diversity of business models that play a part in how patent value is leveraged. This portrait is far from definitive and invites further discussion, which we sincerely hope that readers will engage in. A full screen slide can be found on my blog, *IP Insider**.

It is not only the landscape for monetising patents that is evolving rapidly; so too are the strategies and attitudes towards them. There are more buyers and there appears to be less of a stigma associated with selling to or sharing patents with businesses in a better position to extract value from them. At current count, there are at least seven distinct types of patent monetiser. The myth of the simple patent troll has given way to complex business models (some with their own R&D and internally developed patents); those that acquire patents to combine with their own; and still others that acquire all the assets in their portfolio.

I hope that the patent monetisation landscape provides a springboard for discussion about the differences between current IP business models. I find the differences more compelling than the similarities. Some patent businesses do not sue; some do so occasionally; still others are almost entirely about litigation. Most appear to be well capitalised and some are under the radar. The landscape is more crowded than a decade ago, and it is likely to evolve as even more complex structures for extracting value are created, and as operating companies grow more comfortable with alternative models they can work with.

Businesses are learning that defraying IP-related costs through a rights sale, purchase or partnership can provide valuable efficiencies and increased return without necessarily increasing the litigation risk.

Specialty businesses (call them patent monetisers), representing both non-practising and practising entities, are often in a better position to extract patent value than operating companies, small and medium-sized enterprises or independent inventors. The reasons include the ability to move faster and with fewer encumbrances; more experience; better access to monetisation capital; and added leverage through aggregation.

The reluctance on the part of many holders to allow third parties to extract financial return from their invention rights is abating. Monetisation is more of a necessity than many had initially realised (or were willing to admit). The past 10 years have made it clear that when it comes to generating a return on patents, one type of business strategy will not satisfy all rights or holders. Expect the next decade to offer an even broader range of monetisation styles and options, and a more diverse group of participants to take advantage of them.

* IP CloseUp, **www.ipcloseup.com**

0 to 50 in 8.5 years

2011

When this column started publishing in 2003, IP investing was less of a strategy than an idea. Today, how patents contribute to results is better understood - so are the associated challenge.

Don't let the lofty prices being paid for mobility patents and businesses fool you: while IP rights have made significant gains as financial assets, they are yet to be universally accepted.

When IAM magazine was established, its audience included a small but growing core of innovative IP managers and lawyers. The original "IP investor" column was aimed primarily at them and a handful of non-practising patent owners. Now called "The intangible investor", the column still serves that audience, but has grown to include a wide range of direct and indirect investors, including operating companies with commitment to innovation and R&D.

Despite progress, the role of IP rights such as patents in business performance remains murky. To be fair, these are not easy assets to comprehend, on or off the balance sheet. Context driven and time sensitive, the size, industry, capitalisation and risk tolerance of an IP holder all influence its value. In theory, good patents are worth at least something to everyone. In practice, the mobility mania is showing us that they are worth more to some holders than others. Call it perceived need.

Who? What? How?

Just who is an IP investor? What is considered an IP transaction? How is success or return on IP (ROIP), best measured?

This is my 50th "intangible investor" column. That the column has appeared in every issue of *IAM* is as much a surprise to me as anyone. The editor Joff Wild and I had talked about starting an IP business magazine as early as 1998, while we worked on my book, *Hidden Value*, for Euromoney Institutional Investor. When Joff asked me if I could write a column for the new business journal, *IAM*, I feared there would not be enough material to fill 1,000 words every other month. Now I have more ideas than the publication knows what to do with and some of the spillover can be found on IP CloseUp, an independent blog I started in early 2010.

Accomplishments

What has IP investing achieved over the past decade or so, and what still needs to be accomplished? A few observations:

• IP rights are being taken more seriously by businesses and IP management.

• It's becoming clearer that IP investors come in many shapes and sizes. Some secure patents internally; others acquire them; still others employ them to partner. Fewer investors appear to be looking to make a quick buck on dispute avoidance.

• More people have an interest in IP performance than they may at first appear to; call them IP stakeholders.

• Much to the chagrin of some economists, senior managements are beginning to take Intellectual property as seriously as tangible assets. (Their fiduciary responsibility to investors is yet to be a significant factor. That will probably change.)

The media loves to cover a war. They are especially attracted to patent disputes involving large dollar amounts, well-known companies and the latest technology. IP disputes, in fact, are less frequent and rewarding than we are sometimes led to believe.

Aspirations

A lot still needs to be accomplished:

• IP transactions need to be recognised as more than out-licences. They may include M&A, individual asset sales/buys or securing favourable customer agreements.

• IP performance needs to be better measured. Patent counts and royalty revenue are only part of the performance picture.

• Good IP reporting enhances respect for assets, holders and strategy. Business reporters need to be more thoughtful about sources and their possible agenda.

• An IP dashboard configured to industry needs and business goals can help C-level execs better steer innovation-driven businesses. (Reminder: too much patent data can be less useful than too little.)

• Investors need to scrutinise how IP rights are being used. IP education, information and communication are good for shareholder value. IP disclosure should be seen as an opportunity, not a requirement.

• Patent quality and value are not the same. They are often confused. Investors need to understand the myriad factors that make a mere right and an asset and that allow an asset to be monetisable.

• Patent disputes are inevitable. More efficient alternatives for resolving them are required.

• Business schools need to integrate IP into the core curriculum.

The good fight

IP rights, including patents, are a force of good. They are not an impediment to innovation or a tax on business, as some would have us believe. A positive sense of mission to educate and inform about IP rights will help their progress and keep them in perspective. IP rights may be exclusive for a period of time, but their exclusivity should not put the value they generate beyond the reach of many. An educated stakeholder is potentially a loyal one.

The playing field for deploying IP assets such as patents is levelling. For holders unfamiliar with flatter terrain, it presents a problem of having to deal with new competition. For those previously unable to enforce their rights because of size or cost, it represents an opportunity to provide more value and create new businesses. The intangible investor is starting to materialise. By *IAM* 100, we may have a better idea of what she looks like.

Build, license, buy or steal

2012

Companies that can gain access to the right patents at the right time, regardless of the price, may be in the best position to win in the competitive consumer market for smartphones, cloud computing and social networking.

For some business the high cost of securing valuable patents at the right time, regardless of cost, is crucial not only for the freedom to sell their products, but also to prevent competitors from capturing dominant market share and dictating profit margins. It is a game that many significant tech giants have sufficient resources to play and, in most cases, cannot afford to observe from the sidelines.

Recent portfolio transactions (Nortel, et al) have proved that some buyers are prepared to pay a hearty premium to keep certain patents out of the hands of competitors. C-level executives, boards of directors and activist investors are all fascinated with these marquee IP transactions – not only because of their cost, but also because of their potential for game-changing impact. Management's scrutiny may seem meddlesome, but it is forcing some businesses to re-examine their IP inventory and the effectiveness of their strategy.

Pride of inventorship

Patent holders sell and buy for many reasons – some of which have more to do with financial reporting than IP strategy. A company that may need revenue in a particular quarter to meet Wall Street estimates may choose suddenly to conclude a long licensing negotiation for cash, "If we can get it done this quarter." Other factors include a business's preference to make a one-time licence payment or consummate a patent purchase in a strong quarter, or hide it in a weak one.

Informed IP stakeholders can play a key supportive role in assuring that patent objectives are realised. It is not easy for a chief executive or activist investor to refrain from second guessing IP management about monetising patents when prices are at historic highs. With a little help, however, they can be welcomed as collaborators. Their ability to access capital and manage risk should not be underestimated.

Until recently, companies rarely acquired patents: engineering pride, the belief that costly R&D should be self-sustaining and fear that showing a weak hand may encourage disputes (and firings) forced many prominent IT businesses to go it alone. Why pay cash for innovation rights when R&D and legal departments could churn them out like parts on an assembly line? That is, until companies started taking an honest look at which of their patents actually read on their products and which of held by others' do.

Pay the ticket

Much in the manner of large pharmaceutical companies, more IT companies have concluded that if they cannot successfully generate, in-license or buy patents, acquiring companies that own those they require is not a bad alternative (see Google's acquisition of Motorola Mobility). Businesses in the financial position to pay market prices for the innovation rights and know-how they need to practise, or to prevent others from doing so, will not let them stop them.

For cash-rich companies such as Microsoft (US$57.4 billion), Apple (US$81.6 billion) and Google (US$42.6 billion), the cost to settle litigation or acquire most patent portfolios is little more than a speeding ticket on the valuation highway. It is barely a blip on analysts' quarterly earnings radars. Premium buying beats having to do business in the shadow of ongoing disputes or spending billions to design around. The size and importance of some of these patent transactions have sucked stakeholders not normally associated with intellectual property into the vortex of the patent strategy process. A transaction such as Nortel-Rockstar gets done for many reasons, but rarely without the support of senior managements and boards of directors.

The patent transaction process is not without its ironies. Patents in a distressed sale can frequently command higher prices than those sold when the company is solvent – that is, the patents of some companies are worth more with the company fully dead than partially alive. A distressed IP sale will be orderly and take place according to bankruptcy court rules. The process is more transparent and inclusive, and at the end of the day there will be a new owner – possibly a hostile one. It behoves affected parties (or their representatives) to participate. They can bid on the assets in the hope of acquiring them at an acceptable price or make it more costly for other parties to do so.

A roll of the dice

In solvent sales there is more mystery about who is interested in the assets and at what price. This makes acquiring patents somewhat riskier. It also makes it more difficult for most buyers to sell the deal internally to management and directors. In the case of a near-bankrupt company (e.g. Kodak), there is also the risk of fraudulent conveyance – unauthorised sale of the assets pre-filing – which can unwind a deal faster than a buyer can say "Department of Justice".

For many businesses, abundant R&D and patent filings may be an effective means of innovating, but they are rarely productive enough to fill all of a company's IP needs, especially in patent-intensive industries.

Executives are learning to be less sanguine about their IP resources. When it comes to patents, it is sometimes more efficient to secure what is needed rather than rolling the dice on what a business might be able to generate internally or get away with legally.

While necessity may be the mother of invention, pride of authorship may prove too costly for even the most innovative companies to endure.

The imperfect storm

2012

A new wave of anti-IP rhetoric is angrier and uglier than ever. Figuring out who is fuelling it and why is not that difficult. Overcoming the negative impact is.

Patent and copyright holders that enforce their rights are making a lot of people angry. The convergence of increased competition, blighted economies and misinformation is unleashing a new wave of vitriol directed towards IP rights and owners which is more dangerous than it may appear. Holders and managers who are focused on maintaining their IP rights many also want to think about exercising their First Amendment ones.

The perfect IP storm is about to make landfall. Those already dubious about the use of patents and other rights see an opportunity to cut them down further. Inducing broad audiences to see IP as casually issued monopolies in the best interests of a few is getting easier and, worse still, somewhat fashionable.

Technology and business media are joining with political organisations, some tech businesses, lawmakers and an increasing number of academicians to challenge IP rights. Disdain for patents and copyrights are not new. Its political correctness is. Nurtured by half-truths about IP abusers locking out competitors and shaking-down businesses, many people believe that intellectual assets impede innovation and represent privilege; they are akin to bank bailouts and inflated CEO compensation.

Having been dealt stiff body blows by the courts and recent legislation, IP is on the ropes. Of greater concern than naysayers are IP managers and attorneys who know better, but remain silent.

Occupy Wall Street, the Arab spring, Russian unrest at the election polls and the ascendances of multiple Pirate Parties have raised suspicions about power and control. Faster access to more information has changed the way that people view ownership. You turn on the tap and water comes out. Only expensive restaurants have the audacity to charge for it. You turn on your computer and data streams are now accessible, embodied by content, such as music and images. Ease of access and broad adoption have made collecting tolls appear inherently unfair, like taxing the air.

Not in decades have people felt so removed from those in government and business. Frustration is growing about economic control and IP rights, never beloved, are in the middle of a bloody battle in which millions believe that their personal freedom is at stake.

From an anti-IP perspective, there is plenty to complain about: the high cost of obtaining and defending patents; trolls which are often depicted as blood-sucking parasites; patent sales, such as Nortel's US$4.5 billion auction dominated by cash-laden tech giants; and IP doubters including economists and law professors such as James Bessen, Michael Meurer, Josh Lerner, Michael Heller and Lawrence Lessig, who don't believe that intellectual assets should be treated like other property. They would sooner see patents seriously weakened, if not eliminated, and invention licensing compulsory.

The wide and generally blind acceptance (*Washington Post, et al*) of Bessen, Ford and Meurer's working paper, "The Private and Social Costs of Patent Trolls", is particularly troubling. In this study they argue that non-practising entities (NPEs) are really patent trolls "who opportunistically litigate over software patents with unpredictable boundaries", and are responsible for serious social and economic damage. Using stock market "event studies" around patent lawsuit filings, the authors claim that NPEs were associated with half a trillion dollars of lost wealth from 1990 through 2010.

Bessen, *et al* acknowledge that their work received support from the (ironically named) Coalition for Patent Fairness and research assistance from PatentFreedom. Both of these groups are in turn supported by significant patent holders, fearful of more assertive ones.

Another serious concern is the rapid rise of self-proclaimed Pirate Parties, which in just a few years have been established in more than 40 countries. The first Pirate Party was the Swedish Piratpartiet, founded in 2006. Other parties and groups have been formed in Austria, Denmark, Finland, Germany, Ireland and the Netherlands. In 2009 the original Pirate Party won 7.1% of the vote in Sweden's European Parliament elections and won two of Sweden's 18 European Parliament seats. In 2010 the Pirate Parties International was founded in Brussels at the PPI Conference. In September 2011 in the Berlin state elections the Pirate Party won 8.9% of the vote and 15 seats in a state parliament.

As James Naughton in *The Guardian* reported: "It isn't often that a political party takes a relaxed view of file sharing, advocates radical reform of intellectual property laws, opposes state surveillance in all its forms, evangelises about open source, and then has electoral success in the real world."

Managers and technology investors cannot afford to be complacent about IP rights. They were hard won and, if recent events are any indication, they will be difficult to retain. Those who believe that IP continues to contribute positively to society and commerce need to be more explicit about where and how. An increasing number of people want to see IP rights and their enforcement demonised. They believe they are by-products of government control and special interests, and limit freedom and social welfare. Unheard are the voices of those who know that the IP system, while imperfect, is inclusive and effective.

Driving a stake through the heart of IP rights will not put innovation disputes to rest or give file sharers what they desire. However, with numbers on their side and the world economy in turmoil, IP naysayers are in a good position to gain a foothold. Any one of these developments – the passage of the America Invents Act and weakening of patents, the growth of Pirate Parties, anti-troll trash talk and the global Occupy movement – would not have so much impact. Taken collectively, they are a force to be reckoned with.

If it ain't broke, fix it anyway

2012

Patent suits are down relative to a 29% increase in grants over the past decade; median damage awards are at a 16-year low. So how come everyone and his cat wants to fix the patent system?

The frequency and cost of patent disputes are wrecking business and slowing innovation. At least, that's the belief of an increasing number of technology companies, publications and academicians. The facts, however, show that disputes are way down relative to the dramatic increases in patent filings and grants between 2000 and 2010, and the median award for 2010 was down to just US$2 million.

While patent litigation is more prominent in the media, it is less frequent and impactful than popularly believed. It is not entirely clear whether patent doubters are merely parroting what they hear from infringers and what they read in the press, or promoting an agenda of their own. However, the net effect is the same.

As the playing field has levelled, making it easier but more costly for infringed patent holders to be heard, many businesses that rely on innovation but don't always properly secure it are seeking a more favourable 'incline' – closer to what they are used to historically. Some believe that the America Invents Act is intended to readjust the scales and has made questioning patent quality too easy and legitimate enforcement more arduous.

What is broken in the current patent system is the unbridled detractors who, without presenting all of the facts, depict patent enforcement as inherently unfair and detrimental. Lest we forget, in the eyes of the law, infringing someone's patent - knowingly or not - is stealing.

Headlines such as "Tech Giants Slug it Out Over $2b 4G Patents" excite readers. If patent battles between Davids and Goliaths make for good copy, those between evil Davids and good Goliaths serve a broader readership. It is amazing how many people still buy into the troll myth - a view which is promoted by those with an economic interest as much as by those who think that patents provide too much power. Patents are confusing, and simplifying matters where they are concerned is attractive to some. Few holders enforce questionable patents for nuisance value because the cost and time of resolution have made doing so much less attractive than in the past. That patent enforcement is inherently dubious and financially devastating is not the first lie that confused and frightened people have been asked to swallow. It will not be the last.

There is no argument that patents, the inventions they protect and the related disputes that arise are complex. Determining what is truly innovative and who controls it is not a simple matter. Some honest confusion plays a role in why most people regard patent enforcement as wrong, and royalty payments as an unfair tax. But feedback from the CIPOs, lawyers, asserters, investors and IP professionals whom I talk to suggests that both vested interest and lack of awareness play a part in anti-IP thinking. (If I am preaching to the choir, forgive me. You might forward this column to a journalist or investment banker.)

Patent exclusivity still strikes fear in the hearts of many otherwise intelligent people who do not understand what it means or the various ways it can be positively applied. It sounds worse than it is in practice.

This makes it surprisingly easy to rally public opinion against patents and other IP rights, such as copyrights, which the general public believes are the province of wealthy businesses and smart attorneys, and something they could never benefit from.

Even those who may know better are starting to believe the rhetoric. It has become more fashionable to trash intellectual property than to respect legitimate innovation and innovators. (This is also true of content or copyrights.) Technology publications such as *TechCrunch* and *the Huffington Post* (both now owned by AOL) have been most strident in their anti-patent rhetoric. A sample headline: "Apple Made a Deal with the Devil, No, Worse: a Patent Troll." (You can't make this stuff up.)

Surprisingly little is conveyed about the unauthorised use of inventions – something that goes on routinely. Businesses get away with it largely because they know that SMEs and inventors are unable to handle the cost and complexity of resolving disputes. In a sign of the maturing market for invention rights, investors today are willing to provide acquisition or litigation capital for patents. While some infringers have more to worry about do not expect them to roll over and pay hefty settlements if they do not have to - or without a long and proper fight, and some loud whining.

Infringement that is successfully identified and penalised is a win for innovation and commerce. If infringers do not want to pay the going rate for using the invention rights of others, they can come up with a legal design-around or a better alternative. Building a better mousetrap is what capitalism is all about. However, non-infringing alternatives are easier imagined than created, and are quite costly. For many businesses, the answer is to 'borrow' inventions, especially if they are unlikely to get caught doing so or it is unlikely they will have to pay much if they do. More scrutiny is needed where the patent system is legitimately the weakest: examination; pendency; the difficulty valuing infringement; and the cost and time to resolve disputes.

Is it really that difficult to track what claims a product may be infringing before it goes to market? In the not too distant future, I believe that technology will better serve innovators by automatically linking products sold to the claims that they may infringe, placing the burden of proof on sellers. This will enable earlier detection and less contentious licensing agreements. It will save R&D dollars and render the ignorance defence weak if not obsolete. It will also result in new businesses and higher returns - not a bad thing.

Late to the race, not the victory

2012

Buying late and paying a premium for the patents that a company needs is no longer just a viable IP strategy; it is a surprisingly lucrative one.

The recent moves of companies such as Google, Facebook and Microsoft that have been relative latecomers to patents, and are being forced to play catch-up, are an illustration that they have learned from their early miscalculations.

Once laggards, these businesses are benefiting from a late start, quickly amassing fully embodied patent families that they can rely on now, as opposed to gambling their fate on R&D and patents yet to issue. Balancing the right amount and type of research and patent filings with rights that are in-licensed or otherwise acquired, is a strategy that more businesses are learning to employ. For those that are cash-rich and creditworthy, it can make sense to buy patents after an industry starts to mature if it means securing the rights that they and others need. Overpaying rarely enters into the equation.

In 1996, when I was putting together my first book, *Hidden Value*, Microsoft had just six issued patents. It is hard to believe that an explosive software services company with billions in revenues could fall into this trap. Companies such as Microsoft, Cisco and Apple believed at the time that they could succeed on the strength of their market share, brand recognition and ability to invalidate patents and settle disputes. They all have come to realise that this strategy will only take a business so far.

What some businesses might consider reckless abandon to others is prudent IP management. Microsoft's annual R&D spend is about US$9 billion - more than four times that of Apple. Although that might be a relatively small R and a very big D, it raises a very real question: what is Microsoft getting in return for its investment that Apple is not? Large numbers of patents mean something, but not much if they don't read on the right products. Patents that a business needs to prevent or win litigation, or to influence industry direction, are priceless. Unfortunately, they are only occasionally generated internally.

Microsoft's recent acquisition of some 800 patents and applications from AOL for US$1.1 billion showed it can be decisive.

While US$300 million was the generally accepted value of the portfolio, Microsoft knew the marketplace well enough to pay what seemed like a ridiculous amount and then turn around and sell parts of the portfolio to Facebook for about half that price while keeping what it needed. The fairness of the AOL sale process is not the issue. Microsoft recognised how and to whom these patents were meaningful and how they might be used to neutralise its arch rival, Google.

Patent catch-up can be an effective strategy if a business has the vision and resources to play. The creditworthiness of some companies renders their cost of capital minuscule. Historically low interest rates and an enormous cash position (Apple's is US$110 billion), coupled with the difficulty of converting costly R&D into relevant inventions rights, can make acquiring relevant patent portfolios at almost any cost more sensible than self-generating all of them.

With the AOL transaction, Microsoft went one step further. It effectively became a patent dealmaker, competing not only with operating companies, but also with non-practising entities (NPEs) and aggregators. This is a strategy that only a handful of companies have the sophistication and resources to pull off.

To date, no NPE – not even Intellectual Ventures, with US$6 billion raised – has been able to effect an IP acquisition greater than US$200 million. I can only believe that will change as investors realise the importance of costly portfolio purchases and companies become increasingly willing to collaborate on accomplishing them. Patent management is becoming more of a market-focused enterprise, balancing risk and reward with available cash and timely opportunities.

This is not to suggest that companies can be lazy about conducting R&D and filing patents. They are learning that, like the pharmaceutical giants, it is not enough to go at it alone. Today, no company can generate internally all of the innovation and rights that it needs to compete. IP management (indeed, good company management) demands that many businesses engage in effective R&D, patent filing and licensing, as well as be able to acquire patents and businesses intelligently as risk, cash and market conditions dictate.

Paying a premium for quality is not a unique idea. It could make the game of patent haves and have-nots (and have-maybes) even nastier than it is already. If companies can move faster and speculate more boldly on what to secure, and tap into NPEs and the capital markets to help them, IP management could get even more complex.

To those detractors who believe that this is not real innovation, but mere financial engineering, I say this: if patent transactions are what it takes to get the marketplace to recognise what is inventive and what assets businesses need to succeed, it is a healthy part of an evolutionary process. If small and medium-sized enterprises, independent inventors and investors can benefit from these moves – and I believe that the smart ones can – you can be certain that IP M&A has only just begun.

The benefits to be derived from these transactions, aside from lucrative returns for some sellers, include a new respect for good patents.

Recognition that the rights to meaningful inventions can have significant value, even if they have not yet been upheld in court, reflects positively on the patent system and the growth of IP management. The cold reality of patent deal making may be too stark for some. Still, it beats the cynical game of legal cat-and-mouse that currently pervades the patent world, where important inventions and valid rights, and their holders, are too often denied the recognition they deserve.

Patent wins are overlooked and under-reported

2012

Defining a patent "win" is not as simple as it may appear. It defies easy explanation and differs by industry, company and audience.

Most people regard patent out-licensing as a clear indication of success. Strategic patents, however, typically associated with freedom to sell products, are rarely seen as a win. The double standard is particularly confusing when it comes to operating companies whose primary concern is to maintain market share and profit margins. Businesses that are unable to relate the role that their rights play in performance can expect to pay a price. The inability to articulate patent performance (under-reporting) affects market value and access to capital, as well as reputation for innovation. Many strategic holders whose patents are performing well often fail to explain their relevance because management has not clarified what good IP performance means. Patent wins need to be defined and reported before regulators require it.

Outside of royalty income and enforcement damages, successful patent performance is still a mystery. That is why I believe most companies do an awful job of discussing it, even when it is in their interest to do so. Explaining return on IP (ROIP) can be equal parts frustrating and embarrassing. Just ask most chief IP officers (CIPOs).

ROIP can mean many things to different businesses and audiences. The onus is on the CIPO or equivalent to provide a context to define success and manage expectations. Lest we forget, it is not always obvious why companies conduct research and file for and maintain patents. Audiences want to know that patents are necessary; that they are being used effectively; and that they are providing an adequate return.

ROIP typically represents the net of the costs paid by companies to obtain legal rights (e.g. patent filings, continuations, maintenance and legal fees), and the R&D underlying an invention. In some cases it also may reflect the cost to acquire rights to practise an invention. ROIP for purposes of this discussion is the costs associated with identifying and nurturing an invention, and obtaining and managing the patents that cover it (additional outlays are usually necessary to defend or enforce them).

Out-licensing is the type of IP performance that is readily understood on Wall Street and by senior management. Unfortunately, patent out-licensing is in most cases a fractional revenue generator for operating companies and is often inappropriate because of the pain associated with litigation. It also is only one of several ways - albeit an important one - that patents can generate return. Others include in-licensing and cross-licensing, mergers and acquisitions, patent sales, securing customer and vendor relationships, shareholder value, enhancing reputation and brand equity, and cost of capital.

Interpreting return on defensive intellectual property is much more difficult to calculate than identifying licensing income. Despite this, strategic intellectual property can be more valuable to some businesses than rights that generate direct, high-margin income. It really depends on the particular industry and business model, and on timing. Licensing is readily understood, while strategic patents are typically recognised as useful albeit abstract assets, contributing vaguely to the bottom line.

Operating companies that can step-up and explain subtle patent wins reveal not only performance, but also depth and determination.

For example, patents that can help to make an LCD display sellable with, say, 35% market share with 25% margins are pretty valuable. Which patents are they and how do they play a role in product revenue and overall profitability? How much in the way of R&D, filing fees and legal costs was invested in securing the patents? What is the estimated return to the company over how many years?

IP holders are under increasing pressure to prove the value of their portfolio. As R&D costs rise and the cost of borrowing remains low, buying necessary patents at market prices may be a safer and more efficient strategy for some. Companies that develop patents internally need to justify build-versus-buy decisions, as they do with other assets.

Business executives and boards of directors - many of them graduates of elite business programmes and experienced in running public companies - have been weaned on managing human, financial and physical resources, plants and equipment, people, capital and strategy; not on deploying intangible assets. Intangibles need to be managed aggressively and reported regularly. Companies that are timid about occasionally selling under-utilised intangibles in a carefully structured transaction that facilitates shareholder value without compromising safety may also be underestimating their assets.

A business that conducts little or no out-licensing need not be embarrassed if doing so makes sense given its industry and business model. Conversely, if it has a valuable portfolio of rights that can be monetised, it may want to consider deploying those assets in the form of licensing or sale. Increasingly, transactions are being structured that allow sellers to retain maximum protection, as well as counter-assertion resources and some back-end returns, without direct patent ownership.

It is a reporting challenge to quantify the role that patents play in various with performance. There are many impediments to doing so and precision is certainly one of them. But the attempt still must be made.

Businesses that rise to the challenge can free themselves from reliance on the "trust me" approach to IP management that satisfies few and undermines credibility. Good IP rights deserve better treatment; so do investors.

He's no Robin Hood

2012

File sharing promotes a culture of piracy that makes it more acceptable to steal branded goods and inventions, as well as copyrighted content. Big daddy Kim Dotcom is sticking it to all IP holders.

In the court of public opinion, copyrights and brands have fared poorly. Thefts of digital content and counterfeits are easily achieved and difficult to stop. Patents have not done much better. A cultural disdain for IP rights has emerged, facilitated in part by a range of businesses that stand to profit from free content and illegal access to inventions, lookalike goods, and end users who don't give a damn.

Exhibit A for the legitimisation of IP theft is Kim Dotcom Schmitz. Dotcom Schmitz has slyly built himself into a modern folk hero, complete with mellow gangsta style and outsider reputation (he is a champion video gamer and car racer). This larger-than-life, medallion-wearing bad boy looks like he deserves a modest scolding and a health club membership, not 20 years behind bars. That is what he and his supporters would like you to believe. In fact, his illegal businesses have generated more than 66 million illegal subscribers and have helped to make file sharing acceptable and cripple the recording industry.

Dotcom Schmitz's image is no accident. While it may appear that he is merely taking on the Man on behalf of the public good, he is really part of a larger IP crime mechanism that ignores ownership when convenient and belittles enforcement. Dotcom Schmitz, who has previously been convicted of embezzlement and insider trading and whose net worth is estimated at US$200 million, is no Robin Hood.

Respect for IP rights has reached new lows. While the public may not yet be interested in using patents illegally, many manufacturers of the products that they buy are. Some try to paint patent enforcers in a negative light, calling them names such as troll or predator; others rely on flawed academic research to demean them. Their arguments are no less specious than Dotcom Schmitz's. Some companies infringe inventions unwittingly, but others do so systematically because, like file sharers, they know that the chances of getting caught are slim, the punishment is relatively light and, perhaps most importantly of late, the public frequently does not care.

The piracy economy exists in no small part because a wide range of people believe it is acceptable - even fashionable - to use other people's creative output. Many otherwise honest violators believe they are not stealing, but are merely doing what most PC or smartphone users are meant to do – download, copy and share. Most companies that violate patents are not as naïve as they make themselves out to be. A significant number have concluded that many inventions are merely incremental improvements on prior ones, and are questionable to begin with.

"Megaupload and the twilight of copyright" is an extraordinary article which appeared recently in *Fortune* magazine. It is written by respected legal journalist Roger Parloff, and is essential reading for anyone affected by IP rights. Parloff details how Dotcom Schmitz created a piracy empire that generated hundreds of millions of dollars, and how he may yet escape prosecution. He also puts into context the complex evolution of file sharing and its potential impact.

"At one time," writes Parloff, "Megaupload (Dotcom Schmitz's international file sharing operation) alone accounted for 4% of the globe's entire Internet traffic and was the 13th-most visited site on the web, according to the government, with more daily visitors than Netflix, AOL, or the *New York Times*." Dotcom Schmitz founded Megaupload in

2005 and set it up in Hong Kong, although he himself is a dual citizen of Germany and Finland, and a permanent resident of New Zealand. When arrested on 19th January 2012, he was living in a leased US$24 million estate. The vanity plates on three of his fleet of more than 25 luxury cars read GUILTY, EVIL and GOD.

To date, says Parloff, the only sense of public outrage has been against the prosecutors: "The Electronic Frontier Foundation has filed papers criticizing the government for having, through its shutdown of the site, deprived innocent third parties of access to their files. It also suggests that the seizure violated the First Amendment."

In the 1970s and 1980s many people who went into the field of copyright saw themselves as fighting to help authors, musicians and artists - and therefore as being on the side of the angels. By the 1990s, however, many who entered the field came from tech backgrounds and saw copyright as a constraint to progress.

The *Sony Betamax* decision of 1992 may allow Dotcom Schmitz to escape punishment. This is more than just an outdated law that exempts recording device manufacturers from prosecution. It is part of a larger change in attitude that has allowed an emerging class of businesses and end users to rationalise profiting from IP theft.

Most do not realise that the piracy culture is hardest on little-known artists, authors and innovators. Popular musicians who thrive on live performances can afford to provide free or reduced-cost access to their recorded work. It's an alternative form of advertising and they will recoup recording royalties on concert sales and brand equity. Left out in the cold are the artists who need every dime from every book, song or photograph sale they can generate. Similarly ignored are inventors without sufficient capital to commercialise their work, license or enforce their rights, or to sell them competitively.

IP theft feeds on new ideas, thrives on distribution and prospers on cooperation. The effort to legitimise stealing of creative expression - from songs to handbags to smartphone improvements - is working because a culture of complicity supports it. I am afraid that it will take more than putting Dotcom Schmitz behind bars to set things right.

The need to lead: IBM under the microscope

2013

Obtaining large numbers of questionable patents has been more effective for some companies than maintaining a handful of really good ones. Patent count leader IBM will need to be more creative to stay ahead.

A perennial leader in obtaining new US patents, IBM is also acknowledged as a successful licensor. IBM is not content merely to win the annual US patent count; it believes that it must dominate it in dramatic fashion, as it has every year since 1993. Until recently, few questioned the implications of this strategy. However, with perspectives on patents and performance evolving, portfolio size and effectiveness are being questioned, and volume filers are being subjected to greater scrutiny.

Companies closest to IBM in the patent race – HP, Microsoft and Intel – have each generated thousands fewer patents than Big Blue over the past decade. In fact, 2.5 to 4 times fewer. Companies with comparably huge global patent portfolios, such as Samsung, Canon, Hitachi and Toshiba, tend to deploy their intellectual property more defensively. That three of these businesses are focused on consumer electronics makes business-to-business leader IBM's fixation on annual patent counts that much more unusual.

Brody Berman Associates compiled aggregate totals for US patents granted to leading IT companies from 2000 to 2011. Over this period, IBM (46,292) was granted more than two-and-a-half times as many patents as Microsoft (18,120), HP (17,699) and Intel (17,484) – visit IPCloseUp.com for graphs depicting patent leadership. For 2011, IBM is four times as great.

Lapse rates are difficult to discern, but IBM elects not to maintain between one-half and one-third of the patents it obtains, many within 24 months of issuance. The company also generates direct annual licensing income from patents, trade secrets (know-how) and software-based copyrights, variously described as being worth from US$500 million to over US$1 billion. This accomplishment is especially meaningful given the reputed quality of the company's 34,000 active patents, only about one-third of which are US rights.

Strangely cynical

IBM's approach begs the questions: what is IP performance and how is it best measured for a particular type of business?

Large numbers of patents are thought to be better for providing IT businesses with the freedom to sell products, dissuade enforcement from others and facilitate licences. Also, bigger sounds better. IBM's 'more-is-more' strategy when it comes to obtaining rights has become a dubious distinction of sorts. In fact, the company allows many more patents to lapse than it maintains. It also makes broad use of defensive publications to ensure that certain inventive ideas remain unpatentable and stay out of the wrong hands. With what amounts to a volume strategy, IBM is strangely cynical about patent quality. Originally a hardware company that evolved into a software and services provider, IBM's main business is no longer computing. While it still sells a lot of mainframes and peripherals, how many patents does a consulting firm need to compete? Few of the most innovative businesses maintain tens of thousands of patents, and none of the most successful consulting firms do.

High patent counts impress those in the C-suite and on Wall Street, and may keep some competitors at bay. A portfolio of patents that may not be special individually in quantity may comprise a sufficiently dense thicket to be effective – and you never know when a claim may read on someone else's product, possibly even a client's. Intellectual Ventures has certainly taken a page from this playbook. Some patents are made more meaningful with volume to complement them, reputation to support them and commitment to use them. Patents with claims that read on successful products are more meaningful, but may need to be enforced – a risk that most large holders are still reluctant to assume.

IBM has a history of helping to enable businesses. Its experience and know-how (trade secrets) are valuable resources. In combination with the right patents, they can be extraordinarily effective. Securing a disproportionate number of patents gives a company an aura of prowess that helps to maintain both clients and shareholders. While quantity is not everything, in information technology it frequently means a lot. Whether used as a defensive shield or a revenue-generating sword, a large, diverse portfolio in the right hands commands a certain respect. For individual or families of patents to have real value, they must not only be extraordinary, but must often be enforced.

Top dog

When IBM sold patents to Google and Facebook earlier this year, it was believed that those rights could be worth as much as US$1 billion. Sources knowledgeable about the transaction told me that the amount of the Facebook transaction was more in the range of between US$30 million and US$50 million. What Google and Facebook likely secured, in addition to apparent cover from a small part of IBM's portfolio, was a positive relationship with an IT superpower. This has more to do with public relations than intellectual property, but it was a small price to pay.

The power of cross-licensing, as IP strategist Marshall Phelps explained to Lew Gerstner when the latter was named IBM CEO in 1993, is not readily reflected on a balance sheet. Using cross-licences instead of cash to secure freedom to operate can be highly rewarding to the right company.

For the past 20 years, 'bigger is better' has propelled IBM's patent portfolio strategy. It remains to be seen whether the company has become trapped in its own image as IP top dog, striving for dramatic patent counts at a cost to quality and real return. Securing patents should not be seen as an arms race or blocking exercise. It also should be seen not as an end, but as a means.

Public IP companies – a business model whose time has come

2013

This is likely to be a crucial year for publicly held licensing companies (PIPCOs). Interest is booming as a result of savvier IP investors, better access to capital and better marks in court.

The emergence of IP-rich companies whose shares trade on global exchanges is presenting new opportunities for patent holders and investors alike.

Pure-play licensing companies – non-practising patent licensing companies with a single method of generating return – are being supplanted by more robust business models. Through acquisition or merger with complementary operating businesses, publicly held licensing companies (PIPCOs) are emerging as vehicles that are more easily understood by investors, better able to access the capital markets and more acceptable to the courts.

PIPCOs are no longer simply non-practising entities (NPEs), but neither are they every company with a patent portfolio and licensing agreement.

Investors are realising that public IP ownership can take many forms. Innovative businesses that secure IP rights for defensive purposes via self-funded R&D have given way to enterprises with more synergy and less risk. Critics tend to cut public IP monetisers some slack, generally refraining from labelling them with the 'T' word. Perhaps sharing the spoils of patent enforcement through public ownership and having to make public disclosures is seen as inherently more democratic than individually owned licensing operations, such as those controlled by Lemelson, Katz and Myhrvold?

At last count, no fewer than 27 companies trade on US, UK and Canadian stock exchanges that include among their primary objectives direct patent monetisation. As recently as 18 months ago, all but a few would have been considered licensing-only businesses. The mix now includes enforcement businesses, which joint-venture inventors and SMEs; licensing businesses, which conduct proprietary R&D and obtain patents through filings; so-called privateers, which acquire rights from others, including operating companies that stand to profit; and small companies which sell products and have the resources to enforce patents.

While the patent monetisation business makes good sense, it is not for every holder. Many file suit because the legal system forces them to. Defendants frequently find it more cost effective to drag out a case rather than to settle. Whether their primary premise is operations or IP monetisation, PIPCOs are emerging as a class of stocks that are increasingly attractive to investors and are now followed regularly by IP-aware securities analysts at investment firms, including Davenport & Co, Jefferies, Lake Street Capital, Craig Hallum and Brean Murray.

Capital for PIPCOs is available not only from the public markets, but also from litigation financing firms such as Juridica (see "Patent litigation as an investment class" in *IAM* 56), and in the form of contingency representation from law firms, which have improved their ability to model the risk and economics of patent disputes.

Another reason for the rise of PIPCOs has been the acceptance of patent disputes as a type of public spectacle. Closely watched technology litigations today command an international media audience. What were once considered boring courtroom battles over minute engineering advances are now seen as prize fights between innovation Goliaths (or Davids and Goliaths) that affect people's lives. And there is no lack of experts willing to speculate on their meaning.

With the exception of Qualcomm, Acacia, InterDigital and VirnetX, all with billion-dollar plus valuations, public IP licensing companies tend to be small caps. Mosaid, Tessera, Rambus and WiLAN comprise the next tier, between US$500 million and US$1 billion. The remaining 19 companies are what Wall Street calls micro-caps. These include Vringo, Document Security Systems and Augme Technologies. (See "IP CloseUp" for a more complete list of PIPCOs). Most technology mutual funds and institutional investors will not own them because of their limited float and low volume, which can cause share prices to spike. Micro-caps tend to be owned by experienced individual investors and smaller investment firms and funds with a higher tolerance for volatility.

The lack of broad ownership means that these companies are frequently misunderstood. Most of them are excellent little companies with impressive assets and astute management. But they are also story stocks that need to be explained carefully. If PIPCOs truly are an idea whose time has come, their future depends on delivering on promises, not simply making them. Defensive-minded patent-rich companies such as Microsoft, IBM and Samsung are arguably also PIPCOs, although their huge market cap and revenue streams make them less dependent on the outcome of individual IP disputes.

IP investors today are better able to recognise the managers, rights, disputes and structures that will lead to positive returns. They also realise that for some, better overall return on investments can be achieved when patent ownership is a complement to product sales. This focus is a testament not only to the growing importance of patents in commerce, but also to the maturity of IP management. Since beginning to write this column a decade ago, I have maintained that an educated IP investor is a powerful resource. This has not changed. The PIPCOs most likely to succeed will present performance that goes beyond required disclosure and be able to convey it convincingly to diverse audiences.

Disclosure: Neither Bruce Berman nor Brody Berman Associates holds a position in any of the companies above. Bruce Berman is a principal with Brody Berman Associates in New York which advises public and private IP companies.

Silicon Valley: too big to fail, or too big not to?

2013

Successful tech companies have transformed what was once the cornerstone of invention into a place that is strangely inhospitable to bold ideas and strong IP rights. What will it take for Silicon Valley to get its mojo back?

Driving down Highway 101 or El Camino Real from San Francisco to San Jose, you come upon dozens of well-known businesses – many of them global brands that form the foundation of the information economy. For innovative companies and entrepreneurs, the opportunities to repeat the success of companies such as Apple, Intel and Google have become significantly fewer and further between, and patents are playing a major role.

The pressure is on for new businesses to succeed faster and bigger. The opportunity to try something new and fail with honour – once a hallmark of Silicon Valley – is fading. Moreover, many employees of established companies believe that disruptive technologies can cost local jobs in the short run, even if they may generate more new ones over time. Cynicism is growing towards businesses that are willing put new ideas into practice; so is suspicion of the rights that they secure to protect potentially game-changing inventions and those that control them. No wonder, venture capital investing is down and exit strategies are more limited. Even the private equity's industry's median return has been 6% a year since 2007, far below its historical 13%.

"It has never been easier to start a company, and never harder to build one," said David Lee, a venture capitalist at SV Angel.

David O Sacks, a Silicon Valley executive who sold Yammer to Microsoft for US$1.2 billion last year, summed up the challenges in a post on Facebook.

"I think Silicon Valley as we know it may be coming to an end," Sacks wrote. "To create a successful new company entrepreneurs have to find an idea that has escaped the attention of the major Internet companies, which are better run than before". On top of that, it must be "protectable from the onslaught of those big companies once they figure out what you're on to".

If I hear Sacks right, he is saying that "those big companies" are in the position to take an entrepreneur's idea and run with it (or to quash it), not only because they have the size and capital, but because the patent rights which may protect it are less meaningful and more arduous to enforce.

An aversion

Independent software and e-commerce developers and big tech have something in common: they share an aversion for recognising others' innovation. They typically see patents as threats, not as potential assets that can facilitate success. Surely, broad patents can create a minefield that can make legitimate competitors cringe. But without reliable IP rights, new technologies would be even less likely to evolve and backing for many groundbreaking ideas would be scarcer. The campaign against software and other patents is motivated by a perceived need to neutralise the leverage provided by strong invention rights, especially now that more managers and strategic investors are equipped to enforce them. A patent can be a frightening thing to a business that might be infringing the wrong one.

Ironically, large Silicon Valley companies are being awarded more patents than ever. They are also purchasing them where they can for whatever price they may command (cost is not usually an issue; nor is driving up prices). Increasingly larger portfolios have done little to diminish the Valley's suspicion of strong, litigation-quality patents and those businesses, practising or not, that may own or capitalise them.

Companies that own what may have once been disruptive inventions that are now somewhat mainstream tend to hold on to what they own by managing their assets and minimising risk. To them, patents represent potential threat. Their conservatism may be a boon to margins and market share, but is a barrier to new ideas that could encroach on profitability and threaten their brand. I have no doubt that there are managers at Google who are kept up at night thinking about killer search algorithms or business models that are right now being developed on someone's Mac or PC that could bring them down. Despite owning better than 18,000 of them from its purchase of Motorola last year, patents are something that Google is likely to fear more than embrace. The founders of successful tech companies like Sergey, Steve, Mark, et al are today closer in spirit to 19th and early 20th century oil, steel and rail titans than they are to entrepreneurs.

Hackers' mantra

The hacker's mantra heard often around Facebook, "Move fast and break things," has become more style than substance.

A pre-initial public offering valuation of US$100 billion will tend to do that. "Move fast and break the bank" may be more like it. Patenting and commercialising new inventions is becoming expensive, risky and, as far as patents are concerned, increasingly subversive. Once pioneering enterprises' response to success is to play it safer. Maybe the real innovators have moved to Kansas or Michigan, where the engineering schools are hungrier, the economy more stagnant and the rent cheaper, allowing for a slower burn and longer time line?

Of late, Silicon Valley's activities have been tempered by too much size and paranoia about invention rights. It may take another recession, or tech bubble, and cheaper real estate to get its mojo back. While competition is generally good for innovation, it can also reach a point of diminishing return. Too much pressure to succeed too quickly with weaker rights is a poor catalyst for future return. The opportunity to fail is a key to success.

Patent system's bad actors are not confined to trolls

2013

The headlines proclaim that NPE suits are up and awards paid to them are higher than for operating companies. The reasons why, and who among IP plaintiffs and defendants act in bad faith, can be revealing.

Bad actors that undermine the patent system are not confined to those nonpractising entities (NPEs) with dubious rights and nuisance suits. They include operating companies that are frequent defendants in suits which hold thousands of patents, but perhaps not the right ones. Businesses with insufficient freedom to practise all of the inventions that underlie their complex products have been known to decry those that offer them a licence.

Patent enforcement, distasteful to both defendants and plaintiffs, is an effective if inefficient means of identifying abuse and establishing the quality and value of invention rights. Parties have yet to come up with a more reliable alternative. Businesses such as defensive aggregator RPX and licensing engine Acacia may be moving in that direction.

Data from litigation consultants Lex Machina and PwC indicate that recent increases in patent suits are attributable to NPE activity. Suits filed by patent monetisation entities accounted for 19% of US patent suits in 2007, but that number increased to 56% in 2012. The PwC study found that the median damages recovered by NPEs in patent litigation are nearly twice as high as those of operating companies, but in either case we are not talking about dramatic returns. Over the 2006-2011 period it was US$6.9 million (NPE) versus US$3.7 million (operating companies). The amount of the median NPE award, in fact, is down by 37.7% from 2001-2005, when the figures were US$10.9 million versus US$5.6 million.

While the two studies report increases in the number and value of NPE suits, they do not provide much context.

The last time I looked, there were at least half a dozen types of NPE, only a handful of them acting disreputably, with questionable patents, and banking on the high cost of litigation for a quick settlement. Many NPEs hold good patents that operating companies wish they had secured through R&D or acquisition. Until about 1990, businesses had been able to get away with many patent portfolio mistakes. Quality was less relevant, because it was unlikely to be tested. Today, with patent holders asserting more good rights and with many more valuable rights to assert, the pendulum has swung in their favour. Regarded another way, the rise in patent enforcement is merely the patent system and markets doing their job. For innovation to evolve, it is necessary to require that businesses pay for the invention rights they need to sell a product. For those who have never had to play on a level field, being forced to can seem unfair.

By my count, only a few licensing businesses are what could accurately be referred to as businesses that do not contribute to innovation or commerce. They are frustrating, but they exist less because of weaknesses in the patent system than because of the high cost of patent litigation. This would appear to benefit larger, better-capitalised businesses. Painting all non-practising patent enforcers as trolls is inaccurate and potentially dangerous. Some NPEs settle early not because their patents lack quality, but because – given the economics of patent disputes and the risk of losing even under the best circumstances – early settlement is often a wise business decision. As one astute patent manager told me recently: "Intelligent patent enforcement has become more of a singles and doubles game. Those who swing only for the fences are more likely to strike out."

'Black hat' or bad trolls are responsible for generating the headlines, but not the story. There are at least four reasons why NPE activity is up, and none of them has to do with a lack of patent quality or frivolous patent suits, a term that even President Obama has learned to use. They include the following:

- Patent grants have been rising steadily and were up 27.3% between 2009 and 2010 alone. More useful inventions mean more disputes. (Also, AIA joinder requirements that stop plaintiffs from filing multi-party suits have forced them to file individual ones more often than.)
- Declaratory judgment rulings require a plaintiff to file suit before a defendant can establish a more favourable venue. Many NPEs believe that they must file suit first and talk later. Perhaps even more important, for small and medium-sized enterprises, universities and NPEs to be taken seriously in licensing negotiations, they virtually have to file.

- More capital is available from more investors to fund enforcement activities and more law firms are willing to partner with NPEs, and more options are available, including better access to experienced managers. There also is greater investor awareness of undervalued, un-monetised IP value.
- NPEs simply are better at monetizing patents than most operating companies. Some work with thirdparty or 'privateer' NPEs to achieve their licensing objectives. The stigma associated with patent monetization continues to decline despite the best efforts to cast NPEs in a negative light.

Electing not to license an invention often comes down to a business decision; so too does how patent infringement gets resolved. For many businesses, the risk of – to put it delicately – 'not volunteering to take a licence' makes economic sense. In the unlikely event that an infringer is caught, the potential cost in terms of a settlement or licence is typically is a fraction of the return that has been, and will continue to be, realised. Designing around an invention is extremely expensive and difficult; buying or licensing the patent, too. For many, 'catch me if you can' remains a viable IP strategy; especially in conjunction with 'I had no idea we were infringing someone's invention'.

DC watchdog gets serious about foreign theft of US IP

2013

The findings of the Commission on the Theft of American Intellectual Property are a good start to addressing a global problem with deep local roots. However, the report fails to mention the damage that domestic IP theft is wreaking on the US economy.

"American companies are suffering the loss of hundreds of billions of dollars a year due to intellectual property theft by foreign entities," reports the Commission on the Theft of American Intellectual Property, an independent, bi-partisan group of lawmakers and business leaders dedicated to examining the causes and impact of IP theft on US strategic and economic interests.

The commission provides a beacon of light in a dark sea of anti-patent, anti-IP monetisation proposals circulating in Washington. Its findings are generally meaningful and its recommendations timely. There is just one problem: there is no mention of the damage that domestic IP theft inflicts on the US economy. Co-chaired by Governor Jon Huntsman (Utah, former ambassador to China) and the honourable Dennis Blair (admiral, US Navy, retired; former director of National Intelligence), this

ncludes that US intellectual property – including content,
ɔods and inventions – is under siege by foreign businesses and
...ents, and dramatic measures must be implemented now to halt
the loss of valuable ground in the innovation battle.

In late May the commission released a report detailing its findings, which
include losses of hundreds of billions of dollars a year in revenue and
millions of jobs, as well as a drag on US gross domestic product growth
and innovation incentive. The report states that international IP theft is
not just a problem in China, where it is rampant, but in Russia, India and
other countries, in a worldwide challenge. Many issues are the same: poor
legal environments for IP rights, protectionist industrial policies and a
sense that IP theft is justified by an uneven playing field, which benefits
developed countries.

Kudos to the commission for recognising the importance of IP rights. Its
research is often startling and its recommendations brave. It is difficult to
disagree with the essence of this well-written 89-page report, something
that every IP professional should read. Noticeably absent, however, is a
discussion of the impact of IP theft by US companies on other US
businesses. That would lend credence to the idea that there is a problem
that the US Patent and Trademark Office and the courts have been
unable to address, and that the trash talk about trolls is mostly that. While
domestic IP theft may be deemed less of an act of espionage than foreign
stealing, it is no less a crime and has significant implications for
innovation and the economy, especially job creation.

"IP theft needs to have consequences, with costs sufficiently high that
state and corporate behavior, and attitudes that support such theft are
fundamentally changed," the commission concluded.

The recent focus on frivolous patents suits is largely a distraction
intended to divert attention from the real issue: theft of IP rights,
especially patents, by US companies against other domestic businesses. It
is not the first time I have brought up this uncomfortable subject and, I
am afraid, that it will not be the last. It is unclear how much domestic US
patent infringement goes unrecognised and how sincere an effort

businesses make to identify and license potential patent holders before products are sold.

In a *Washington Post* editorial, Blair and Huntsman wrote:

"Equally as important as the current situation is the potential for future damage. Our intellectual property is what provides the new ideas that will keep the U.S. economy vital and productive over the long term. If less innovative foreign companies can reap the profits of U.S. research and development and innovation, we will lose our competitive edge and eventually experience a decrease in incentives to innovate altogether... The United States must make the theft of U.S. intellectual property both risky and costly for thieves."

Amen to that. The same could be said of domestic patent infringement. The commission's recommendations include denying products that contain stolen intellectual property access to the US market; restricting use of the US financial system to foreign companies that repeatedly steal intellectual property; and adding the correct, legal handling of intellectual property to the criteria for both investment in the United States and for foreign companies listed on US stock exchanges.

The chairman of the House Permanent Select Committee on Intelligence, Mike Rogers (R-Mich), has hailed the report, saying it makes an important contribution to the discussion about the danger that IP theft poses to US economic wellbeing. "I heartily agree that Congress and the administration need to act quickly to help American companies defend the hard work and innovation that is the lifeblood of our economy," Rogers said in a statement.

Foreign IP theft may indeed be a greater problem for the United States and other developed nations than theft by domestic companies, but the threat is no less insidious; potentially it is even more damaging. Education will help, but strict and even punitive measures may be necessary to get infringers' attention. Currently, innovation and intellectual property are being threatened from without and within; frequently, by some of those who may appear to be on the leading edge of it. We need bi-partisan organisations such as the commission to identify unauthorised IP use, quantify the dangers associated with it, and help enact legislation and provide systems that prevent it from further eroding healthy competition.

IP theft is not only a problem emanating from foreign businesses and governments. It poses a domestic threat that the courts and the patent system seem ill equipped to address. Let us hope that the United States can rise to the challenge and recognise that systematic IP theft is an economic tsunami in the making which needs to be taken seriously at home as well as abroad.

Explain thyself

2013

Can a handful of small, publicly traded companies play a significant role in how the IP value and performance of larger businesses is measured? Yes, they can.

A group of businesses, some valued at below US$100 million, are helping to turn what were once under-utilised, off-balance-sheet IP rights into an asset class worthy of global investor interest. Be assured that the scrutiny that these companies command will not exist in a vacuum. While larger IP holders have resisted embracing the higher levels of transparency required of recently public licensing companies, soon this may no longer be an option. Public IP companies (PIPCOs), which can range in size and differ widely, are a catalyst for examining patent performance. They present a case for all patent holders – operating companies and non-practising entities (NPEs) alike – to show that while the meaning and value of their IP rights may differ from business to business, they must still be measured. PIPCOs shed a light not only on how audiences and markets look at all IP rights, but also on how they can be used to achieve objectives.

Many of the recent PIPCOs are licensing-only models that are the product of reverse mergers, a faster and less costly way to go public and access equity markets. Some see that the timing is right to leverage patents' enhanced status, particularly when prices for even mediocre families are going through the roof. PIPCOs' remoteness from counter-assertion makes them attractive to investors. They also possess experience that operating companies lack for managing patent disputes and negotiating 'stick' licences.

Like it or not

PIPCO performance will inevitably have an impact on larger, IP-rich companies, even if their strategies differ. The inability of operating companies to identify and otherwise unlock and explain the value of their costly R&D and patent portfolios is a growing burden. These new companies are a reminder that innovative businesses can be grossly inefficient when it comes to deploying inventions and rights and explaining their benefits. PIPCOs' presence also illustrates the increased vulnerability of many tech giants to selling products that infringe inventions which they do not own or have a licence to practise. And – much like biotech and entertainment companies before them – PIPCOs have a good story to tell.

For most businesses, IP transparency provides more benefits than impediments. It can help to boost holders' return and investors' profits, and is likely to lead to more and better innovation. However, there is a flipside to increased disclosure: it makes failing to inform audiences about results or to be inconsistent in reporting them more difficult. Companies that are not used to being held accountable for their IP performance will find that there is more pressure to explain their performance. Data will need to be maintained and compared, and promises kept.

For public companies with significant IP rights, value is often poorly reflected on the balance sheet. Businesses tend to be secretive about how (or even whether) their invention rights generate return. A sea change is taking place about how patents are regarded, deployed and, ultimately, communicated to stakeholders. It will cause patent holders of all sizes to rethink not only what they reveal about their intellectual property, but how they do so. Not all holders agree that they can be held to the same IP performance standard as licensing companies. Most believe that it is inappropriate for them proactively to convey IP strengths and reveal some weaknesses rather than obscure them under huge patent counts. If businesses must disclose their financial performance, why shouldn't they be required to reveal their IP results?

To be fair, few businesses have the same IP goals. Larger patent holders are often more focused on establishing design freedom and preserving market share and profit margins than on generating licensing income. They also are reluctant to sue customers or vendors, and are fearful of countersuits. For this group, the IP performance metrics are more complex. With PIPCOs, NPEs and others generating direct cash flow from patent licensing, it is a formidable challenge for larger tech businesses to show how their costly R&D/ IP model makes business sense.

Exceed requirements

PIPCOs' meagre revenues and thin market values can magnify the impact of single patent licence or settlement. This is in contrast to the disputes between the likes of Apple and Samsung. No matter who wins or how large the outcome, the impact on either party will be negligible. Like many attractive investment propositions before them, not all PIPCOs will succeed. Some consolidation in the sector is inevitable. No doubt the public IP company terrain in five years will look different from today. Hopefully, it will be a little easier for audiences to understand. Investors typically have short memories and are susceptible to good stories. However, as they become better informed about intellectual property and learn which managers actually deliver, and which businesses consistently produce, they will become more difficult to impress. Regardless, increased attention to patents and patent strategy will not go away.

PIPCO disclosures must occasionally exceed requirements. I tell my patent-rich clients not to meet disclosure, but to take a leadership role in exceeding it. As long as sharing information does not compromise their competitive advantage or weaken potential litigation, they are on safe ground. Investors are smarter today. IP success is no longer a 'trust me' proposition for the terminally confused.

Value and performance must be explained, and respect earned. For smaller patent holders looking to make a mark with licensing revenue, and for larger patent holders protecting profit margins, the first rule of IP reporting is the same: under-promise and over-deliver.

Microsoft: bold IP moves provide intriguing results

2013

Failure to dominate in diverse product lines has not stopped Microsoft from crafting an innovative and sustainable patent strategy, and generating billions of dollars.

Microsoft has taken more heat over the past 20 years for what it has not achieved than any technology company.

Missteps in product development and market strategy have slowed its once meteoric growth and hampered its shares. Richard Sherlund, a Microsoft analyst at Nomura Securities, estimates that the company has lost about US$17 billion from missteps in its online and search engine businesses. But while the company has managed to get only some businesses near right, it hit the bull's eye with at least one: intellectual property. When it comes to IP management, Microsoft - a laggard with just 300 patents and applications in 2003 - has quietly become a world leader. It has established a formidable patent portfolio, a successful licensing programme and a willingness to move swiftly when the opportunity arises.

Microsoft is a highly profitable company with high margins and more than US$85 billion in cash. Unfortunately, less than perfect may not be enough in hyper-competitive tech markets, where second place may just as well be last. Microsoft has a video game console (Xbox), a dominant web browser (Explorer), a major web portal (Bing), a corporate software business (Office), an operating system for personal computers (Windows) and cloud computing services. The company is a mish-mash of businesses in which competitors such as Google, Yahoo!, Oracle, Apple and Nintendo specialise.

Patent bridge

What the giant software company does far better than all the others is secure and monetise IP rights. Microsoft - a company that I and many others have never been a big fan of - has transformed itself from a once Evil Empire into a truly innovative IP business, with multiple ways to generate superior returns. It is among the few large holders of patents, capable of deploying them without litigation, as well as using them to deflect it. The once 97-pound IP weakling among tech companies that everyone seemed to push around has built itself into a confident leader without the use of performance-enhancing drugs. Closer to IBM's IP management model than Qualcomm's, Microsoft prefers to use patents less contentiously, as a bridge to facilitate business relationships. It has filed two patent suits which were settled: one against TomTom and the other against Barnes & Noble. Microsoft has successfully defended itself multiple times in suits that sought significant damages, and has made several large IP purchases or investments (for a summary see IP CloseUp.com).

With 40,786 patents, Microsoft is just behind Samsung and IBM for top patent recipient. It reportedly generates as much as US$8 for each Android handset sold worldwide to about 20 vendors, and about US$10 on Nokia's. Microsoft could generate US$8.8 billion annually from Android royalties alone by 2017.

With softness in its operating divisions, Microsoft is headed toward an even more IP-focused business model, and as such is a proponent of strong patents. At Microsoft, IP is "the tail that wags the dog." While Google, Cisco and others would like to see patents weakened or disappear, the Bill Gates founded enterprise believes that its future is tied to them. Its R&D spend is US$7.4 billion for 2013, among the highest of all companies. This may be a small R and a big D - more of an accounting strategy than a tactical one - but it speaks loads for how seriously Microsoft takes new ideas. Microsoft's future has been much debated. Some argue that breaking up the now slow-growing company and selling the parts will generate a better return for shareholders. While that may be true, it still manages to rank with Philips, IBM and Qualcomm as one of the smartest and most profitable operating companies for IP rights.

Profit engine

It is unlikely that Microsoft will perform the same magic in its operating divisions that it has in its IP business. It's a tough act to follow. What its diverse IP success portends is a smaller, even more highly profitable company - one that conducts abundant R&D and selective M&A, sells several types of products but profits most from its intellectual property rights. Cash-rich Microsoft has shown that it is not afraid to make bold IP moves, including patent acquisitions. It is easy to be granted a lot of patents; it is much more difficult to secure those that are worthwhile for the right price and know how to orchestrate a proper return on them.

All that Microsoft really needs to do is to spin off some divisions or to manage them wisely and allow the profit engine, IP rights, to kick in. Do not be surprised to see it take a page from Qualcomm's playbook. The majority of Qualcomm's revenue comes from baseband chips, which connect phones to cellular networks, sold to wireless device makers such as Samsung, Apple and HTC. The bulk of the company's profit comes from the licensing of so-called code division multiple access technology, a radio-communications standard used in other chips, handsets and phone systems.

It would be wrong to call Microsoft, with its many operating units, a non-practising entity. It would be right to say that it is an IP business with prodigious returns derived from patents, some of which it actually practises. Unlike Google and many of its big tech brethren, Microsoft respects patents and would like to see them fully valued. Paying Nokia US$2.17 billion over 10 years for access to its 30,000 patents, and taking over its Qualcomm licences, may turn out to be the bargain of a lifetime, especially if Nokia does the dirty work for Microsoft by enforcing them against companies which are not yet licensed.

War between 3D printing and IP rights is not inevitable

2014

Self-manufacturing almost any product or part will soon be a reality. How rights holders respond will determine the future of many industries and businesses, and maybe of intellectual property itself.

The expiration of several key three-dimensional (3D) printing patents in February 2014 will test the mettle of manufacturers and IP systems worldwide. The ability to create and download a 3D printing blueprint by scanning an object will permit unprecedented copying and raise a host of patent, copyright and trademark questions. This development will affect not only luxury items and toys, but also precision instruments, aircraft parts, weapons and human organs.

While 3D printing makes it easier to create new objects and personalise existing ones, it could also make counterfeiting products as commonplace as music file sharing. That is, unless rights holders choose to liberalise their definition of copying or identify better ways to monitor, enforce and license it. Until fairly recently, expensive 3D printers were exclusive to high-end design and engineering businesses.

Now, they are starting to reach the homes of hobbyists and others, and have the potential to change how many objects are created and distributed.

All of this raises complex legal issues. The Sony *Betamax* and *Napster* cases provide a glimpse of what is likely to occur on a much larger scale. These disputes made clear that in the digital world, value is tied to the ability to copy and distribute. There is little jurisprudence to provide guidance for how IP laws will apply when 3D printers enter the mainstream and both businesses and individuals begin manufacturing items for personal use or for sale. A 3D scanner can render the exact dimensions of an object in a digital blueprint, which can then be uploaded for sale. That means that objects from handguns to pharmaceuticals – many of them patented and subject to copyright and other laws – could be readily produced and sold. Such activity may soon be routine and will be difficult to stop.

Earlier this year, researchers at Princeton University created a functional ear using a modified US$1,000 ink-jet printer. They said that the ear has the potential to hear radio frequencies far beyond the range of normal human capability because the tissue was combined with electronics as it grew in a petri dish. The first 3D printed organ, a human liver, is expected in 2014. China has committed almost US$500 million towards the establishment of 10 national 3D printing development institutes. In 2013 Chinese scientists began printing ears, livers and kidneys with living tissue. Developments unveiled at the 3DPrintshow in London in

November 2013 included medical advances that can be used to create parts with specifications for individuals. This is said to make the process safer and more efficient.

The opportunities in 3D printing are abundant and there is a significant role for IP rights if holders and their advisers play their cards right. Along with investors, they need to learn from past mistakes in the digital world. Partnerships that facilitate collaboration with designers, printer manufacturers and/or users may make sense.

It sounds exciting, but at the same time frightening. Not all IP holders will be thrilled if their rights are easily ignored and readily devalued, and investment becomes too risky.

This brings me to an important paper now available in draft at www.IPCloseUp.com and scheduled for publication in the *Georgetown Law Review* later this year. "Patents, Meet Napster: 3D Printing and the Digitization of Things" was written by Deven R Desai and Gerard N Magliocca of the Thomas Jefferson and University of Indiana School of Law. I urge anyone affected by IP rights to read it.

The authors argue in their heavily cited and well-written treatise that 3D printing should not be subject to existing IP regimes and should be "lightly regulated, lest we make the same mistakes as in the past". Some academics have made similar arguments for software and other intellectual assets. The authors explore how 3D printing will disrupt patents and other forms of intellectual property that have relied on physical limits to prevent infringement. "The promise of 3D printing," they say, "is that people will be free to make almost anything they want themselves, which opens the door to a new wave of innovation from the home, the start-up, and large firms."

They conclude that Congress should assist the dissemination of 3D printing by limiting the infringement liability for personal use in the patent sphere and clarifying the standards that govern digital intermediaries for patents and trade dress. (It should be noted that Desai served as academic research counsel for Google in 2013 while on leave.)

Much of what Desai and Magliocca say makes sense, but it is difficult to regulate (or deregulate) a technology prematurely without knowing what it is capable of or how it might otherwise be enforced. For investors, 3D printing will no doubt be an opportunity, but advocating for weaker IP rights may or may not be the answer. Digital encryption or watermarking schemes that would restrict unauthorised distribution of 3D printing blueprints might be.

However, the lesson painfully learned from music file sharing and the Internet is that once the genie is out of the copying bottle, it will be difficult to stuff her back in.

We know today what we did not know some 20 years ago when Napster ruled the Internet and broadband barely existed: regulating digital technologies under IP law is no simple matter, but it can be done without impeding growth or stifling creativity. Less reliance on the letter of the law may help in some cases of personal abuse, but so will more literal interpretations when it comes to large-scale copying and distribution that competes directly with IP holders.

Acknowledgements

The Intangible Investor and its predecessor column, *IP Investor*, would not have been possible without the support, perspective and patience of a lot of people. They include reliable friends, attorneys, financial analysts, inventors, clients, colleagues, investors and family members.

At the top of the list is Joff Wild, both friend and colleague, who has the confidence and trust to allow me to run naked in the pages of IAM, and the good judgment to prevent me from making a fool of myself. It's been a good decade. I hope there are some more down the road.

Others important to producing these pages include Mark Argento, Rob Aronoff, Keith Bergelt, Francine Berry, Joe Beyers, Don Boreman, Bob Bramson, Elvir Causevic, Fiona Cheung, Manus Cooney, Paul Coster, Dennis Crouch, Doug Croxall, Peter Detkin, Todd Dickinson Paul DiGiammarino, Charles Eldering, Scott Frank, John Garland, Jim Haggerty, Peter Hardigan, John Harvey, Bo Heiden, Brian Hinman, Peter Holden, Gerald Holtzman, Chris Israel, Myron Kassaraba, Rob Kramer, Ron Laurie, Dooyong Lee, Steve Loeb, Bryan Lord, Ken Makovsky, Dan McCurdy, Kazie Metzger, Peter Misek, Judge Paul Michel, Emmett Murtha, Daniel Papst, Russ O'Haver, Ulf Petrusson, Rudd Peters, Marshall Phelps, Steve Pinkos, Brenda Pomerance, Irv Rappaport, Jeff Ronaldi, Ted Sabety, Ron Schutz, Joe Sommer and Ally Xing.

Special thanks to IAM magazine and the IP Media Group.

About the author

Bruce Berman is a strategist, business consultant, author, editor and lecturer focused on innovation and understanding the rights that protect it. He is a principal in Brody Berman Associates, a management consulting firm he founded in New York in 1988 that advises patent and other intellectual property holders, managers and investors about strategic communications and reputation. Bruce works closely with IP holders and service providers in the U.S., Europe and Asia, and has counseled many IP executives, litigators and dealmakers, and their clients.

Bruce is responsible for four previous books on IP and business, *From Ideas to Assets, From Assets to Profits, Making Innovation Pay* (all John Wiley & Sons) and *Hidden Value* (Euromoney Institutional Investor). Articles, chapters and reviews by him have appeared in more than 100 periodicals and books, *including Nature Biotechnology, The Book of Investing Rules* (FT-Prentice Hall), *IP CloseUp*, a popular blog that he publishes, and *IAM Magazine*, where he is on the editorial advisory board.

He is a member of the Intangible Asset Finance Society, Intellectual Property Owners' Association, the IP Hall of Fame Academy and the editorial board of LES *Insights*. Bruce has taught cinema studies at Columbia University where he completed his masters' degree and the course work for a Ph.D.

www.ingramcontent.com/pod-product-compliance
Lightning Source LLC
Chambersburg PA
CBHW060334200326
41519CB00011BA/1932